Don't File For Divorce Just Yet

What You Must Know First

Don't File For Divorce Just Yet

What You Must Know First

CHERYL TAYLOR

www.doistayinthismarriage.com

Copyright © 2014 by CherylTaylor. All rights reserved. This book or any portion thereof may not be reproduced or used in any manner whatsoever without the express written permission of the publisher except for the use of brief quotations in a book review.

Printed in the United States of America

First Printing, 2014

ISBN 978-0-9912668-2-1

Cheryl Taylor Books
324 Main Street
#222
Laurel, MD 20707

For more information please visit:
www.cheryltaylorbooks.com

For Mom, Donna, Lisa and
"Sweet Corn"

TABLE OF CONTENTS

ACKNOWLEDGMENTS	1
Introduction	7
PART I	**11**
It Begins With You	13
1 Faith, Prayer, and Meditation	17
2 Gratitude	31
3 Healthfulness	37
4 Face Your Fears	43
5 Do What Gets You Through	47
6 Meet Your Needs	51
7 Are Your Needs Getting Met Today?	55
PART II	**59**
Making the Decision	61
8 Follow Your Dreams	63
9 Is Your Life Better Because of Him?	67
10 Pros and Cons	71
11 Is That Us?	77
12 Violent Communication	87
13 Trial Separation	95
PART III	**101**
Staying	103
14 Money	105
15 Sex	117
16 The Little Things	121

17 Your Man and His Emotions	123
18 Accepting What Is	125
19 Learn to Love Your Man Again	129
20 Communication	139
PART IV	141
Uncoupling	143
21 Emotions	145
22 Children	153
23 Moving Out	157
24 Finances	161
25 Legal-Eaze	169
26 Learning to Live Again	177

ACKNOWLEDGMENTS

"Let every soul be subject unto the higher powers."

ROMANS 12:13

There aren't enough pages or words to express my gratitude for the love and support owed to those who made this book a reality. I will start with simply thanking God, whose power allowed me to create this book. Spirituality is the only word I can find to explain the force that compels me to write.

I am grateful to my sons, Daren Alexander and Essien Smith, who bring an uncommon meaning to my life. Their kindness, curiosity, brilliance, beauty and strength are what I cherish most about them.

A great amount of thanks is owed to my grandparents, Mary and Smith Johnson. My grandmother, who guided my life for 28 years, gave me a love of writing, through all the letters she wrote me. My grandfather gave me the gift of unshakeable optimism, and an entrepreneurial spirit.

My mother taught me to always have fun, to travel and to read, for which I am grateful. My father did not live to see me graduate law school or finish this book, but he was proud of my role in my 6th grade play, so I know he's smiling down on me now. I love both of my parents, and recognize how challenging it is to raise a creative strong-willed child.

My sisters—Donna and Lisa, and their husbands, Clay and Shane—have been a reprieve for me over the past two years. They've opened their hearts and their homes, which means more than I am able to say. Kellee, Shahara and Lindsey, are my three wonderful nieces, who have three wonderful children. It is truly a joy to watch them as mothers. I am grateful to each of them. Madison and Q, I love you guys too.

My extended family is huge, and provides a consistent source of love, strength and joy. Only Howard University, can throw a party like my family. For all the fun and love I owe big thanks to my uncle Freddy, a.k.a., "Sweet Corn." I also thank my aunts Catherine and Laura, whose lives have taught me the importance of kind, consistent and unconditional love.

To list the names of all my beloved cousins would fill the first chapter of this book. I will mention Joyce, Janet, Fred, Jeff, and Bubby—you guys have known me since I was a kid running around with high-waters and a snotty nose in Chester, PA.

I have a host of girlfriends from Howard University, where I spent some incredible years learning about life, love and the pursuit of happiness. Many of my closest friends are also my sorors from Alpha Chapter, Alpha Kappa Alpha,

Sorority, Inc. We have an uncommon bond that started in the quad, on the yard and continues today. These women taught, and continue to teach, me the meaning of excellence and the power of friendship. Thank you guys for always keeping it real—straight, no chaser—Cindy, Tracey, Maria, Diann, Lil' Kim, Mel, Renae, Chanda and Carolyn. Noah's mom—thank you for being a living reminder of the power of a good vision board.

Thank you Annette, Chris, Ruth and Ellsworth for all those summers at the beach where I was reminded that the best is yet to come and that true love really lasts forever.

I thank Bishop T.D. Jakes for sharing his gift at FBCG, where he preached a sermon so powerful that it cleansed my spirit—giving me the power to clear my mind, body and soul in order finish this work. Tremendous gratitude is owed also to Pastor John K. Jenkins, Sr., who created a spark in me that has only yet begun to burn.

From Baltimore to Utah to India, there are professionals to whom I am in awe of for their kindness and professionalism—David Fax, Robert Mercer, Christine at First Editing, Bhuvnesh and his team, and Blaine at Vervante.

Cheryl Elizabeth Taylor Washington, DC
April 2012

What You Must Know First

My Prayer

God I ask that I may not disappoint myself

That in my action I may soar as high

As I can now discern with this clear eye

BY HENRY DAVID THOREAU

INTRODUCTION

One shovel at a time. That's what I told myself as I shoveled out from under the worst snow storm Washington, DC had seen in decades. I had just left my husband, and looking back now, the snow was symbolic of all the emotions I'd have to shovel through before I got to clarity. I'd never shoveled snow before. He'd always done that. For a minute, just one minute, I regretted having left him in winter.

Still, as unprepared and confused as I was, I regretted the time of year I left him—not the fact that I left him. So somewhere inside me, I knew my decision had not been made in haste; still the unanswered questions flooded my head.

Could I have planned better? Was this the right time? Can I really shovel all this snow with a utility shovel? These were my thoughts as I surveyed the white mounds of snow that blanketed my doorstep, the sidewalks, my car, and everything as far as I could see from the front door of my new home.

Alone, single, hung over from too much red wine and dressed in layers of anything I could find, I cried a little as I pushed my utility shovel into what felt like clay instead of snow. It wasn't until I'd shoveled enough to see my front steps that I realized that I might just see the sidewalk again, and then maybe even my car. One shovel at a time. It was then that I realized that I might just make it through this horrific snowstorm, and if I could make it through that storm alone, then maybe, just maybe, I could make it out here on my own as a single mother.

Yes, moving 30 inches of snow alone can be life altering, but it caused me to believe in me again. The me that went to law school. The me that ran my own bankruptcy practice. The me that survived two miscarriages within six months. Yeah, that me. The strong one. That storm wreaked havoc on us all, but it also brought with it an opportunity to regain my confidence and resilience—qualities I'd forgotten I possessed.

Even though I had my confidence back, I had no idea what to do next. I'd already left, so I did not have to decide that. But, now what? I knew I would survive, but I wanted to thrive—to be the best I could be. The truth is that I hadn't even written a check for an electric bill in 15 years. I was not prepared to leave, and so when I did I was scared and filled with doubts. This is no way to make a life- changing decision. So, I did what I do whenever I'm in doubt—I prayed. I didn't even know what I was praying about. Then it came to me. I needed clarity—clarity to figure out if I had made the right decision, to figure out my finances, to make the right decisions about my life as a single person—clarity about everything.

So, yes, I made it through the storm outside and the one inside of me. I have no doubt it was prayer that led me through this difficult time, then faith, then love of my children, family, and friends—and then intense reading in my local library. Yep, God helps those who help themselves. So, I did what I do best; I started researching and reading to find answers. I started reading everything I could so that I could learn about myself, about what went wrong in my marriage, and about how to get myself and my children to a healthy and whole place despite the divorce. What I couldn't find in a book, I learned by trial and error. So I started writing down what I learned, which became the basis for this book.

Soon after I finished my manuscript, I began to procrastinate. I let the book sit… and sit, and sit. Then one Sunday morning, I got the urge to attend church services. I was new to the area, and had been meaning to find a church home. I have never been an early riser. So one morning about 10:30am I started searching the internet for nearby church services. I found one that had a noon service. Right up my alley. So I went to the church, the First Baptist Church of Glen Arden. The service was wonderful, the choir magnificent, and then the minister appeared. I listened to his sermon and about half way through I heard him say that somebody out there in the pews had a book that needed to get published. I don't think God could have spoken to me any clearer. After that service I went home and began writing with the knowledge that I had learned something out there shoveling that snow and in all the months since, and that it was time to share my knowledge with others who just may be traveling the same path. I believe that God gives us talents to help make our journey a little easier.

Remember, when the going gets tough—and it will—take it one shovel at a time.

Cheryl Elizabeth

PART I

It Begins With You

THE ANSWER WILL APPEAR WHEN YOU ARE READY TO SEE IT

Don't File For Divorce Just Yet

IT BEGINS WITH YOU

Before I made the decision to leave my relationship, I noticed that once a month I would cry in the shower. That was my first clue. I'd dry off, wipe my eyes, and remind myself that I had no reason to be unhappy. Sounds like PMS, huh? I don't want to tell you how long it took me to realize that it wasn't solely my PMS that was making me cry, but my relationship.

Eventually, the tears began to come more than once a month and I realized that I really was unhappy and had to do something about it. Deep in my soul, I knew it was my marriage; I knew what the issues were, and I knew that we had been to counseling several times. Still I pretended to be happy, not consciously— unconsciously. I'm so good at denial that I can even fool myself sometimes. After all, I had everything I needed to be happy right? I had a beautiful home, nice cars, a perfect job, and a husband who provided for me and the children. I should have been happy— damn near ecstatic. That's what everyone told me. So why wasn't I? What I did not know was that there was a cost to pretending to be happy and burying your relationship troubles in the sand. It is called sanity and peace.

A few years after our second counseling attempt had failed, my unhappiness began to rise to the top like an inchworm in a pot of collard greens. No more was I sailing along holding it all in, going along for the sake of my kids, the neighbors, my co-workers. Eventually, it all came tumbling down and hit a point where things had to get better or I had to leave for my own sanity. I fell into a very deep depression, which is highly unusual for me because most of the time I could chair the optimist club.

Depression can eat you alive, from the inside out. I know. I grew up in a small town where I'd seen first-hand what happens to depressed women who let their unhappiness fester. I watched these women engage in multiple affairs, addictions, trouble with children, you name it. As a child I did not know what their sorrows were. Now though, looking back some 35 years later, the root cause of their troubles was their unhappy relationship with their husbands. The thought of these women, and my sorrow for and allegiance to them, somehow guided me in my search for answers after I'd separated from my husband.

I remember one point, years before I decided to leave, when I was having doubts about our relationship. We had compatibility issues that were really weighing heavy on me. So, I headed to a major retail bookseller in search of answers. I wanted to know how you know whether you should stay or go. My search was futile. I left the store despondent and desperate, miserable, with two young children and no answers.

I decided not to go. The timing wasn't right

and I wasn't even sure I wanted to leave. I didn't just sit there though—I had a few glasses of wine and long conversations with my girlfriends. After that I started to do something that would change my life. I began to work on myself. Instinctively, I knew that I needed to start with me. My husband was not the cause of all of our troubles. Nor was he the cause of my unhappiness. I was responsible for my own happiness and before I went anywhere, I was going to have to take a long hard look at myself.

I didn't know it then, but working on me made me better prepared to make well thought-out decisions—decisions that I would not later revisit with regret or sorrow—decisions that would be in the best interest of myself and my children.

In the chapters that follow, you will find all the information and tools that I used to get my head straight before making a life-changing decision. The first chapter deals with gaining spiritual strength through prayer, meditation, and faith. The remaining chapters deal with gratitude, healthfulness, doing what gets you through, addressing your fears and learning to meet your own needs. I know you bought this book expecting an answer to whether you should stay or go, but you know as well as I that you will have to come to the answer on your own. The answer is in you, not in this book. This book can help you pull that answer out of you, and give you confidence in your decision. You, however, will have to do some work. Part of that work is preparing yourself to make the decision of whether you should stay or go. To do that, you will need some tools. That is what this section is about, providing you with the right tools so that you are in a good place to make a life- changing decision.

If you are anything like me, you may be tempted to skip this section and head straight to the section on how to make your decision. Don't do it. Wait. I was forced to wait because I didn't have a resource like this book to utilize. Instead, the answers came to me through life experience. You don't have to go through all that I did. However, if you can find the patience to do the exercises, you will find that your load is lightened, your mind is clearer, and you have strength for a journey that only you can take. Remember it's not just about making a decision, but making the best decision you can make. So, read on sister!

1

FAITH, PRAYER, AND MEDITATION

In the days that I first separated from my husband, I can remember doubting myself about whether I was really going to survive being single again. I had never run a household on my own with two young sons. My confidence level about myself and my ability to live as a single mother was at an all-time low. It was the start of the holiday season, and I was emotionally and physically exhausted and not looking forward to facing my first Thanksgiving without my children. We'd split the holidays so I would have them over Christmas and he had them for Thanksgiving. This felt terrible because I'd been inseparable from my sons from the day they were born. I knew I wanted to separate from my husband, but I had no idea about the indescribable emptiness, loneliness, sadness, and grief that would follow when my sons were not with me every day as they had been since birth.

During one of those lonely dark moments, and there were many in the beginning months of my separation, I thought back to 1998. That was the year I had two miscarriages. I was devastated. We'd tried to get pregnant for two years, and then we did, only to miscarry—twice. The first miscarriage came a month or so after we returned from a two-week trip to Africa. The women in a small African village in the Ivory Coast placed beads around my waist, performed a traditional dance, and quietly assured me I would be pregnant very soon. They were right. I was pregnant within weeks of our return home. I was ecstatic.

I miscarried, only to get pregnant a month or so later.

After the second miscarriage, even the nurses in the operating room at John's Hopkins Hospital felt sorry for me. It was the second time I'd been in the hospital's recovery in four months. I can remember them talking to each other about me as I lay there in recovery, slowly coming to. "Poor thing, she was just here." I remember rolling over and replying that I was going to adopt a baby very soon. They were too sad for me to realize that I was serious. I was groggy, but clear about what my next steps were going to be.

Following the miscarriages, I went into a deep depression for several months. My sadness was a combination of shifting hormones and genuine grief—grief deeper than I'd ever felt. I thought I would never get through this period. I cried and cried. There was no comforting me.

Out of control, that's how I felt. I had no control over losing my babies. Until then, my life had run according to plan: college, law school, husband and... children were supposed to come next. It was my own linear thinking that probably made my loss that much more painful. It never occurred to me that I had been fortunate; life had rarely interrupted my plans. Then again, that meant that I was woefully unprepared when it did.

It was only through an internet chat group that I found some solace by sharing my story with other women who had experienced the same loss. For some reason, I did not have the faith I have now. So I can't tell you that I relied on my faith, because sadly I had none.

During this time I grew to realize that I wanted to be a parent, whether the child grew inside my belly or someone else's.

God answers prayers. Soon after the miscarriages, we were able to adopt a beautiful baby boy. As if my heart wasn't already filled with joy, less than two months after my oldest son came home, I realized I was pregnant with my youngest son, giving me two where there had been none. There is no expression for how happy they made and continue to make me.

It was this time in my life that I often thought back on whenever I began to doubt whether I had what it took to make it out here as a single mother. The lesson I learned is to have faith and believe that God will get you through, even when you can't see how.

DEVELOPING FAITH

If you've been in a long-term relationship with someone, then there is generally some co-dependency, which happens naturally. It is this co-dependency that can sometimes diminish our faith in our own ability to stand on our own or make decisions that are in our best interest. My understanding of faith is that it is the belief in things unseen. I understand it to be like the wind—you can't see it, but you know it's there.

The kind of faith you need right now is faith in your ability to make the right decision for your family. The following few principles outline methods to help with faith and self-confidence.

BELIEVE

Believe, believe, believe. Believe in yourself and your ability to find an answer that is right for you, your children, and your husband. There is an answer just for you, and it will come to you—but you must keep on believing in your own ability to make the right decision.

POSITIVE THOUGHTS

Stay positive even when you want to kick the

ground and cuss at everyone in sight! Turn your thoughts around. Take it from me, negativity will do nothing for you except make you feel bad, slow your thinking, distract you, and block your blessings.

One way to stay positive is to write down all your thoughts for a given day. Once your thoughts are on paper, examine them. Now read your thoughts aloud. You can even tape record yourself saying your thoughts so that you can hear how negative they may be. If they are mostly negative, write a positive statement for each negative statement that you listed. Keep doing this for a week until your thoughts are mostly positive.

BE DETERMINED

Be determined to find the answers you seek about your relationship. Even when it seems like an answer will never come and things will never get better, keep on praying and believing that this too shall pass. The reality is that an answer will come to you, maybe not at the exact day and time you would like an answer, but one will come to you. That's how God works. He may not be there exactly when you call him, but he is always right on time.

STAY IN THE WORD

Staying in the word means making and keeping the spiritual rituals and commitments you have made to God and yourself. It wasn't until I began to stay in the word regularly that I really began to receive the answers I sought and my life began to take on some semblance of order. Here are some ways you can stay in the word:

Read a spiritual book daily—For me, initially, it was of course the Bible, and then the Tao Te Ching, interpreted by Wayne Dyer. For you it may be the Quran.
Attend Religious Services—Visit the house of God. There is something about being in the house of God every once in a while that can restore and retain your sense of faith.
Keep a spiritual or religious symbol nearby—For me it is a small white stone Buddha figure placed on a counter where I can see it from most angles of my living room. It soothes me and centers me.

PRAYER AND SOLITUDE

I would not be writing this book if it were not for the doors of the Catholic Church always being open. I never knew what that term meant, "the doors are always open." It means that the

Catholic Church provides a sanctuary for anyone, anyone at all, to come and bow your head and pray to God. If you don't believe in God, I urge you to pray anyway, and anywhere. For me, it just happened that there was a huge steeple that I could see clearly from the 10th floor window of my office in Washington, DC. I suppose the church and the beautiful steeple called me, but somehow I found myself at St. Dominic's Catholic Church, on my knees at least three times a week during my lunch break. It was the prayer and the silence that helped me clear my mind to make a decision to face the tough road ahead. The constant prayer gave me faith to believe that "this too shall pass," and it did.

It was out of sheer desperation that I wandered into St. Dominic's Catholic Church. I had been to counseling, which was helpful, but I needed something more, something deeper on a spiritual level. I needed to know that I was going to be okay, really. So I started out by praying for clarity. That's all, just some good old clarity. I'd pray to any Saint I could find. I eventually settled on Saint Jude because Jude is my maternal grandmother's maiden name, and plus a huge statue of St. Jude was near the pew where I prayed. I also liked St. Jude a lot because I learned that he is the Saint of hopeless causes, and boy did I believe that my cause was definitely hopeless.

I've always prayed at night, by myself and with my sons. One added benefit to all my praying is that it led my youngest son to pray every night.

If I put him in to bed without praying, he would say, "Aren't we going to pray tonight?" Our prayers have become our special time together. My oldest son caught on to praying early, which eased my mind. Just knowing that both of my sons can comfort themselves through prayer and meditation is a true blessing.

I also noticed that as soon as I get on my knees and bow my head, I feel a sudden sense of calm. It's almost as if my body is trained to relax when I get on my knees.

Besides praying on my knees, I also relied heavily on Wayne Dyer's book, Change your Thoughts—Change your Life. This book focuses on the Tao Te Ching, which is a book that has been translated more than any volume in the world, except for the Bible. For me, just reading the verses, and then Mr. Dyer's interpretation, was a kind of prayer.

At first, when reading the verses in the Tao, it felt like I was learning a new and foreign language. In a sense, I guess I was. I never gave up, and after about a year, I looked back at my life and realized that my thinking and my life had changed for the better. For example, one big change was learning to appreciate life even when things are not going my way, to just be grateful that I am here and well. This was a powerful lesson for me that I learned from the book. So I would strongly recommend this book as it has a tremendous amount of life lessons that can really help you with this period, or any period, of your life. The verses in the book can be life changing if you read them carefully and with an open mind.

Here are excerpts from a few of my favorite verses in the Tao Te Ching:

Because the sage always confronts difficulties,
he never experiences them

—63RD VERSE

This simple verse reminds me to always stay in the moment, and to take life one moment at a time, confronting issues as they come up, rather than waiting until they become huge problems.

The female overcomes the male with stillness,
by lowering herself through her quietness

—61ST VERSE

This sounds a little submissive at first, but it actually is very profound. Sometimes if you just quiet yourself, you would be surprised how your partner will follow suit. It is impossible to argue with someone who will not argue back. Practicing this verse helped me through my divorce by getting me and my husband to a place where we could eventually co-parent in harmony, without the stress and fighting that some couples engage in. Even though we are not together, we are able to co-parent our children in a way that has allowed them to thrive in every aspect of their lives. Stillness, quietness, and peace may be hard to envision and practice while you are going through marital problems, but I swear by these principles for the ultimate welfare of your children; they are the ones who benefit from seeing their parents act civil and kind towards each other.

There was no way that I could have survived this journey without bending down on my knees before God. So whether you call him (or her) Allah, Buddha, Krishna, God, or a Higher Power, just get to praying. If you don't believe me, just try it, you have nothing to lose and everything to gain.

Hopefully, you already have a prayer practice, but if you do not, please remember what your knees are for. Even if you feel like you have so many problems you don't even know where to start, just get on your knees, look up to the sky, and give thanks that you are alive. An answer will come to you in time, if you listen hard, honestly, and frequently enough.

MEDITATION

Meditation sounds so mysterious. It's really not though. The only thing mysterious about meditation is how it works. And it does work. It works to calm your mind and restore your soul. You will need a calm mind and a restored soul as you make decisions about your relationship. You can mediate anywhere anytime by simply closing your eyes, taking a few very deep breaths, relaxing your shoulders, and emptying your mind. I tend to meditate right before I go to sleep at night. It seems to clear my mind and ready my body for a good night's sleep.

Here are two of my favorite meditation practices. The first one is what I call the Beach. If practiced regularly, this meditation can really help you feel better about yourself and everything going on around you. It won't solve your problems, but it can put you in a better frame of mind to solve your problems. I urge you to try it. Last year I did this meditation with my closest friends while on a trip to Miami. They loved it, and hope you enjoy it as well.

THE BEACH

Lay flat on your back, close your eyes and take five deep breaths. Your stomach should rise with each of the five breaths. Release each muscle in your body, beginning with your toes and ending with your shoulders. Let your mind take you to your favorite beach. See yourself lying there flat on your back. Feel the grains of sand as you inch your body into the sand, all the while spreading your arms out like an eagle. After a while, get up and walk toward the ocean. Hear the waves. Walk into the water until it is waist high. Stand in the water, greet the sun and feel its warmth all over your body. Breathe in the warmth of the sun. Feel it surround you and give thanks that you are alive and that all is well. When you are ready, open your eyes.

COLOR FOCUS

Another one of my favorite meditations is what I call Color Focus. Color Focus really helps to focus your mind and clear your head if you stick with it. I often practice this one right before I get out of bed in the morning. As soon as I wake up, I lie there and do not move. After I digest my dreams from the night before, I clear my mind and then picture any color I feel like. Once I have the color, I then imagine the color to be a shape. For example, I might picture a blue triangle in my mind, or a yellow circle. Being able to see shapes and colors is really important because many people dream in black and white. Once I mastered the shapes and colors in my mind, I then started to imagine words such as "happy" in a particular color.

This practice centers me in the morning, otherwise my thoughts are racing and all I'm thinking is: "I've got to do this. I've got to do that, go here, go there…" The ten minutes I spend meditating in the morning calms me and helps me focus on what I need and want to do, instead of all the many things I'd like to do.

These meditations were adapted from one of my most precious books, What We May Be, by Piero Ferucci. I encourage you to read this book because the meditations can be life changing.

Don't File For Divorce Just Yet

2

GRATITUDE

Yes, gratitude is so important it deserves its own chapter. Make no mistake, to make the healthiest decision about your relationship, you will need to have a strong sense of well-being, which you can accomplish through gratitude!

Gratitude is associated with the word grace and it is one of the strongest emotions on earth. I know you may not feel grateful for anything right now. It may be hard to even find one single thing to be grateful about some days, but stay with me on this one. Giving thanks daily works. I can attest to it personally, and there are numerous studies that prove gratefulness increases wellbeing. The results being that people who practice gratitude are happier and less stressed.

Think about it, couldn't we all use a little more happiness and a lot less stress, whether we stay or go? So how do you get grateful, when you honestly and truly believe that you have nothing to be grateful about? The best way is to start from where you are. Start by being thankful for what you have in your life right now.

I discovered the idea of starting from where

you are during one year when I was overwhelmed in my marriage. I had a three year-old and a four year-old, marital problems, and financial concerns. I needed to get a job quickly and put my sons in pre-K.

To top it off, a woman from North Carolina decided to stalk me. She'd found my ad in the yellow pages and convinced herself that I was her lawyer. She'd call almost every day talking gibberish saying that I was her lawyer. I had never met the woman. Then one day she called to say that she was coming to Washington to see me. That's when I contacted the Sheriff's office in her town. The Sheriff assured me that the woman was harmless. It turns out she went to high school with him. He promised to tell her that I was not her lawyer just because she saw my ad in the yellow pages. He also shared with me that the woman had recently lost her teenage sons to gang violence. My heart sank after the sheriff's revelation. I stopped feeling sorry for myself and gave gratitude for where I was in my life at that moment.

This incident was around New Year's, so this became my New Year's resolution. I decided to just start from where I was right there, instead of constantly thinking about where I wanted to be, and what I wanted to have. This attitude allowed me to stay in my marriage another six years, which I do not regret.

So take a few minutes and make a gratitude list, by listing anything that you are truly thankful right now.

1.

2.

3.

4.

Review the list every morning and evening before you go to bed. Within a week or so, you will soon notice that you are a little lighter in your step. Make no mistake, I am not making light of your relationship issues; I have had my own, believe me. But, nothing says you can't feel good while deciding what you want to do. The better you feel about yourself, and your life, the greater the chances that you will make a decision that is right for you.

The gratitude list works because it helps you appreciate what you have right now in your life. It is very empowering to know that at least some things are working right. Gratitude practice helped me with a low point in my own life. I can still remember sitting in my favorite chair and somehow, from somewhere, I got the message to just "start from where I am." What that meant to me is to just give gratitude for what I had at that time in my life. I didn't know the benefits of practicing gratitude, only that if I wanted things to get better, I would need to begin where I was at that moment. From that point on, I never looked back and began giving gratitude for everything every day. Many times I will even find myself at church just giving gratitude, not even asking for anything at all. Just giving thanks. I notice that it is those moments that I spent in gratitude that I have felt totally refreshed. No, my prayers were not instantly answered, but I felt at peace, contented, and happier than I did before I gave thanks.

If you have trouble developing a gratitude list, the list below is based on an exercise called The Attitude of Gratitude—The Gratitude Exercise. It was developed by Catherine Pratt at www.Life-With-Confidence.com. The exercise asks you to repeat the phrases below. You can also make up your language. The idea is that you find something to be grateful about. So go ahead and take a shot at it.

- "I am so happy that I didn't lose my fare card for the train today!"

- "I am so happy that my sons aren't bickering this instant!"

- "I am so happy that I have I have friends who love me!"

Make up your own, or say the ones above. Just figuring out what makes you happy can put you in a good place mentally and emotionally.

Another thing you might try is developing a gratitude book. I'm an advocate for any practice that involves writing, so I gave this one a try, and guess what…it works!

Here's how you can make your own Gratitude Book:

- **Decorate a Journal:** Purchase a journal-type notebook that reflects your personality. The notebook might have your favorite color on it, or you can paste a favorite picture on it. Do what you can to personalize the journal with colors, photos or items that make you smile whenever you see your journal.
- **Give Gratitude Now:** Soon after you wake each morning, write down 3 things that you are currently grateful about. My gratitude list includes that fact that I have wonderful children, a hilarious 70-year-old mother who I talk with most days, fun and supportive friends, a guardian angel that works overtime, a lovely home and great co-workers. Just writing that sentence lifted my spirits. Now develop your own list by using the left side of the page for the gratitude now items.
- **Give Gratitude for the Future:** On the right side of the page, write down 5 things that you will be grateful for in the future. Choose goals that you want to achieve in the future and be grateful for them in the present moment. Feel the emotion as if you have already achieved your goal and

visualize yourself in the picture.

This exercise is powerful because it helps to keep you in the present. So much of the time our minds are focused on everything except right now, which allows us to forget that the present really is a gift.

3

HEALTHFULNESS

I was born a size 14. Really, I don't ever remember wearing any other size, unless you count my sophomore year in college when I starved myself down to a size 6 so that I could wear all the great clothes my best friend's mother sent her from the Texas fire sale. Me and a size 6 lasted for all of about a month and I was right back where I belong.

Today at 47, I love my size. It fits me. I love the swell of my breasts, the curve of my waist and full hips. It feels good not to be on the diet train for once. I rode that diet train since sixth grade, so it was well time to end the trip. These days it's my body that guides me as to how much to eat, and not my mind. I eat only when and what my body needs. No more am I a slave to that voice in my head telling me to eat like they are about to stop growing food.

It wasn't always like this. For years, before and during my marriage, I was a compulsive eater. Then I was an emotional eater. Food was my addiction and it clouded my thinking. The highlights of the day for me were breakfast, lunch, and dinner. Oh yeah, and that 2 o'clock snack, which was usually something chocolate and gooey.

Looking back, I now realize that when I began to address my marital issues, my food addiction released me. No more crazy cravings or eating until I went belly up. I just remember getting on the scale last January and realizing that I was 12 pounds lighter. Disbelief washed over me. Was the scale broken? No, I had just bought it. Then I thought about it and realized that my clothes were looser. Yes, I'm still a size 14, but a real one not the kind where I have to squeeze into spandex anymore, because I'm really a 16 or an 18. Looking back, I probably shouldn't have been shocked. After all, I had visited a nutritionist earlier in the year and she recommended that I push my eating up earlier in the day, eat every 3 to 4 hours, and bring more food to work. I made those changes, which were easy. Then I also took a strength training class twice a week at the gym at my office. I also committed to myself that I would not torture myself with trying to lose weight while going through a marital separation. Soldiers don't fight two battles at once, why should I?

The other thing that really helped me was something I did on my own—I started listening to my body and what it was asking me to eat. No I didn't hear voices. Not right away anyway. Just kidding. Really though, I noticed that my food needs followed my monthly cycle. In the first two weeks of my monthly cycle, I noticed that I wasn't very hungry. I took advantage of this and ate a lot of salad, chicken, and a little else of whatever I wanted. I would just stop eating as soon as I felt the first signs of satisfaction. The second two weeks, my appetite would gradually increase, but my body mostly desired turkey, pasta, yogurt, seafood, spinach, and chocolate. I found that if I fed my body the foods it wanted, then we were both much happier.

Why am I telling you this? Because I know from watching Oprah, and having sisters, that I am not the only one that likes to eat. So, if you have a weight challenge, try addressing the issue by visiting a nutritionist to get some helpful advice. Then practice listening to your body for signs of when and what it really needs to feel nourished. For example, if it's near my period and my mind is telling me to get in my Acura, drive two hours to Philly and scarf down a Cheese Steak, then I know my body is craving iron (steak) and calcium (cheese). My mind just associates these things with steak and cheese rather than spinach and yogurt. After all, I grew up outside of Philadelphia where they make real cheese steaks. So, be kind to yourself in regards to how, when, and what you eat, particularly now.

If you feel you must focus on your weight at this time, I strongly recommend The Appetite Awareness Workbook, by Linda W. Craighhead, PH.D. I've read every diet book known to man, and this is the best "un-diet" book you'll ever find. It's phenomenal because it teaches you to follow your own internal biology when making eating decisions, rather than external stimuli. Another book I swear by is Eating Mindfully, by Susan Albers, Psy.D. I can almost guarantee you will improve your relationship with food and yourself if you spend time with either of these books.

In addition to not dieting at this time, I'd recommend getting a physical, if you haven't had one in the past year. Make time for it because you want to be on your "A" game, whether you decide to stay and work on your relationship or whether you decide to head out the door. Did I get a physical before making my

HEALTHFULNESS

decision about my relationship? No. Did I wish that I had gotten a physical? You bet. I was going through peri-menopause and low on estrogen. In other words, my head felt like it had cotton in it while I was trying to make some serious decisions. This was not cool, at all. I couldn't think straight to save my life. It was nothing but God that carried me through. It wasn't until months after I'd already separated, at my annual GYN appointment that I was diagnosed with early menopause. Oh, that's what those 2 late periods were about? My doctor put me on a low dose birth control with just enough estrogen to make me wonder who turned on the lights. You can't even imagine how great it felt to be back on my "A" game. I was on a roll. It's just too bad I didn't have that little pill while I was trying to deal with relationship issues... Still

I do not advocate taking hormones for more than a few months. I am not a doctor, but I come from people who believe that menopause, generally, is a natural process to be experienced in its entirety—hot flashes, mood swings, confusion, and all.

You get the point. If you haven't done so this year, get a physical please.... You'll be glad you did.

Don't File For Divorce Just Yet

4

FACE YOUR FEARS

All of us are scared of something, probably not the boogey man, but there is something that frightens each of us. For me it's rejection and fear of change, not admirable traits for a writer, but they are my fears and I'm keeping them! The most important thing I learned about fear is that it is just a message telling you to look before you leap. Fear doesn't mean don't leap, just that you better take a good long careful look before you do. That's it.

Fear can't talk, walk, or bite! It took me a long time to realize this, but it's true. The best way to get at your fears is to look them straight in the eye, admit them in the mirror, and keep on moving.

Relationship issues can be especially scary because they can bring up emotions and issues that we are uncomfortable dealing with, and are often connected to our upbringing in some way.

If you are having relationship troubles, you might be experiencing some of the fears listed below:

1. Fear of intimacy.

2. Fear you don't deserve your partner.

3. Fear he may not love you if he really "knows" who you are.
4. Fear you may not love him if you really let him in.
5. Fear that if you talk about the issues, the relationship could end.
6. Fear of being single and alone.

7. Fear of changing anything about the relationship.

Explore these fears and see if you recognize yourself in any of them. If you have these fears or other fears write them down and explore your thoughts on paper. These types of fears are not uncommon, but you cannot fully give and receive love until you have faced your fears.

This next exercise can help you address, and eventually eliminate, your fears. Start by making a list of four of your most unpleasant memories, from childhood and adulthood.

1.

2.

3.

4.

Now close your eyes and vividly remember each of those events. Spend about five minutes on each incident. Then make a list of the emotions you felt during each of these events. This process will help you get at what your fears are. Once you know what your fears are, you are ready to feel the fear and eventually you will release it. Just make sure you actually feel it first, otherwise it will stay with you. Be patient. You may have to do this exercise several times the first few days, but your fears will dissipate once you shine a light on them and allow your body to feel the fear rather than blocking it out or resisting the fear. Start by closing your eyes and paying close attention to all of sensations in your body. My fear comes on me in my belly. My stomach tightens and I feel a heavy feeling, like a hot boulder is inside there. Where do you feel your fear? Allow it to come. Once you feel the fear, breath into it with all of your breath.

Stay with your fear, continue to breathe into it. After a few minutes or so, imagine that the fear is dissipating. You will eventually feel renewed. This exercise is based on an exercise call "2x2" in one of my favorite books, The One Thing Holding You Back, by Raphael Cushnir. I encourage you to read his book for more on fear and other emotions in general.

It's important to feel and release your fears, because if you don't, they will weigh you down and cloud your thinking. Also, change, of any kind, big or small, is scary as all get out. So learning to get your fears in check will help you on your journey, whether you choose to stay or go.

5

DO WHAT GETS YOU THROUGH

In the 9th grade, I was insecure, overweight, and my parents had just divorced the year before. It was then that I discovered how writing and exercise soothed my spirit. We didn't have any counseling, so I gravitated towards these areas instinctively. I started writing and running every day. I don't even know what I was writing about now. I just started writing and somehow I came through that period intact.

If you could use help remembering what gets you through tough times, or you want to clarify your thoughts, I encourage you to take a few minutes and list major life events, and what coping mechanisms you used to get you through.

As I mentioned, a major life event for me was my parents' divorce. The tools that carried me through were exercise and writing. Even today, whenever I have something that seems too big to handle, these two things get me through just about anything.

With regards to your relationship, it is important that we as women develop and maintain adequate coping skills and support networks; often times our own lack of coping skills and self-created isolation masquerades as "man trouble," when in fact the trouble is primarily within ourselves.

Here's a list of some ideas that can help get you in a good place to make life decisions.

- **Reconnect with old girlfriends**—I happen to have a lot of really smart friends from college and law school. I had lost contact with many of them while I was trying to be a perfect wife and mother. Big mistake. No one is perfect, not even me. Lucky for me, when I gave up trying to be perfect, my friends were still right there waiting to accept me as I was.
- **Get an acupressure massage**—This type of massage can release kinks as well as an expensive hot stone massage. You can usually get these quick massages at your local mall, for about 1 dollar per minute. You'd be surprised how good you feel afterwards.
- **Get a manicure**—Just looking at pretty nails can brighten my day.
- **Call a friend**—I love to connect with friends and family by telephone. If I have five minutes, it brightens my day to hear a friend's voice.
- **Do a 10-minute exercise video**—What a pick-me-up! If you do 10 minutes in the morning and 10 at night, you will notice a big

difference in how you feel about everything, including your relationship.
- **Play a game with your kids**—Children are naturally fun, so just connecting with them can go a long way.
- **Start an internet business**—This can be a big endeavor, so really think about this one. I'm mentioning it because it can be really empowering to start a business. I started a business selling purses on the internet. Someone bought my website in less than a year. It was fun while it lasted, and I made some money. Your business should be about you and something you enjoy.
- **Join your local Parent Teacher Association**—There's no better way to get your children to see the seamless connection between school and home than to join the PTA. I was president of our PTA when my sons were in elementary school, and it really helped them in every aspect, including their grades. Being a member of the PTA can also help you develop good relationships with your children's teachers, and help your children develop increased confidence in school, which are always good things.
- **Volunteer for a political campaign**—I have volunteered for three campaigns. This is just so much fun because you are volunteering for something or someone you believe in. Also, the campaigns don't last for very long, so you aren't obligated. Whether your candidate wins

or loses, you are likely to feel a great sense of accomplishment. My sons campaigned with me for a local candidate, which is something I will always treasure and I believe that they will also.
- **Play adult sports**—I'm still looking for a good sports team in my area. I'd love to play kickball, but they are all filled. Adult sports, such as kickball, soccer, or even football can be a lot of fun. Just being part of a team can really be a boost.

I challenge you to create your own list, and revisit it as you grow because your interests will inevitably change over time.

6

MEET YOUR NEEDS

In John Gray's book, How to Get What you Want and Want What you Have, he talks about the need to fill your love tanks. Filling your love tanks is important because sometimes when we get what we need, we often find that our marital problems can dissipate. This is not always the case, but you can certainly benefit emotionally by filling your love tanks. It's important to make sure you are meeting your own needs so that you are not blaming your partner for areas where you can meet your needs.

The exercises below can help you explore and identify ways that you can fill your own love tanks.

SPIRITUALITY

Before I got married, I read the Bible religiously, but my husband and I did not share the same religious beliefs. I eventually stopped reading the Bible and attending church. The end result was that I was spiritually depleted. That is a terrible place to be because there is just no real joy without some sort of spirituality. There is no getting around it, believe me I tried.

I now know that I am responsible for nurturing my spirituality at all times, no matter what goes on around me.

Make a list of ways that you can practice your own spirituality. Some ideas are going to church, reading a religious book, watching a church service on television, meditating, praying at night, and listening to inspirational music at home.

1.

2.

3.

4.

Challenge yourself to do one of the items you listed on a weekly basis, or even a daily basis if you are able.

PARENTAL SUPPORT

Who doesn't feel like they could have used more love from their parents? The reality is that, in most cases, our parents did the best they could. Parenting is hard and it doesn't come with an instruction book. If you have issues with a parent, make a list of ways that you can address those issues.

1.

2.

3.

4.

Another option is to write a letter to your parent(s) identifying what you wished they would have done differently. You could also write an apology letter to a parent if you believe he or she could have behaved differently. You might even consider visiting a counselor if you have serious issues, with one or both of your parents.

FUN

Okay, fun is relative, but you get the point. Get out there and do something you consider fun, something you really enjoy that causes belly-aching laughter.

For me it's just hanging out with my kids and my friends. I happen to have very, very funny children and friends. They make me laugh and I am restored just by the laughter. It doesn't matter where we are. I also love hanging out with my sons, traveling, kayaking, dining with friends, riding my bike, going to beach, double dating, and playing black jack.

Now make a list of things that you have done in the past that were fun and exciting:

1.

2.

3.

4.

Now make a list of items that you would try for fun if no would laugh or call
you crazy:

1.

2.

3.

4.

5.

Great! Now post the list on your refrigerator or in your desk drawer at work. Then actually get out there and do some of that fun stuff.

7

ARE YOUR NEEDS GETTING MET TODAY?

Are your needs being met—right now, today? If most of your relationship needs are being met, then you stay; if not, then you either find a way to get your needs met, or make the decision to move on. I know it is not that easy. I get that it will take work, whether you stay or go. That's just the cold hard truth. The good news though, and there is good news, is that I also know you are not afraid of work.

Each of us has different needs in a relationship, at different times. That's why it's important to evaluate your needs on where you are today, not where you started out in your relationship. Ideally, your relationship grows as you grow, but that is not always the case.

You can evaluate your own needs by writing a list of what you need out of a relationship at this time in your life. For example, I need someone who listens to me, someone I have great chemistry with, someone with sex appeal, a great sense of humor, someone who keeps their word, someone who is kind and loves me for me. Physical attractiveness, a positive attitude, and dependability are also important to me. These qualities are non-negotiable for me when selecting a relationship.

Make a list of the top six things that are important to you in a relationship. Be very careful in writing your list. Make sure these are the things you need for your mental and emotional well-being in order to be happy in your relationship. Be brutally honest and remember it's your list. It should be based only on your needs, not some cookie-cutter idea of what a relationship should be about. Really take your time and develop your list.

TOP SIX THINGS THAT ARE IMPORTANT TO ME

1.

2.

3.

4.

5.

6.

Now that you have the list, take time and write out why each of these things is important to you.

Next, compare your listed items to your present relationship. Are you getting your top three relationship needs met? If not, here are a few ideas:

1. Reevaluate your list.

2. Work on getting your needs met in your current relationship.

3. Find healthy ways to get your needs met outside of your relationship.

4. Consider moving on.

QUICK TIPS

- Develop faith—You'll need it whether you stay or go. Trust me on this one.
- Pray—Get on your knees. Turn your relationship over to God. Then get up and get to work.
- Develop gratitude—Say thanks in the morning and at night for a constant lift.
- Practice healthfulness—Honor your body's hunger signals.
- Identify, feel, and release your fears—You'll be glad you did.
- Stay current—Make sure your needs are getting met today.

PART II

Making the Decision

YOU ARE THE CAPTAIN OF YOUR OWN
SHIP, NOT EVERY SHIP IN THE OCEAN,
BUT THIS ONE FOR SURE.

Don't File For Divorce Just Yet

MAKING THE DECISION

No regrets. That's what we're aiming for here. So, hopefully, you were able to complete at least some of the self-work in the first section. If so, your head should be a little clearer and you are ready to do the work of deciding whether to stay in your relationship.

The chapters in this section contain a series of exercises designed to assist you in figuring out which way to go. The exercises were carefully selected to increase your chances of making a decision that will help you thrive on this journey called life. By making a well-thought-out decision, you increase the chances of creating a life you've always dreamed about. It's your relationship. It's your decision. Own it. Make sure it's fully formed with a balance of intuition and reason. You can't possibly control your partner, but you can control you. Always remember you are the captain of this ship, not every ship in the ocean, but this one for sure. Steer it, guide it. Make a decision that works for you. Life is not a dress rehearsal, and all we have is now, today. So, kick back and get to the business of deciding your future.

8

FOLLOW YOUR DREAMS

In Judith Orloff's book, Emotional Freedom, she stresses the importance of relying on your dreams for guidance. When I first read her book, I really did not think that it made a bit of sense to lie down and ask for clarity from a dream. Truthfully, I thought she was nuts. I mean, I didn't think it could be so simple, but I'm adventurous so I decided to give it a try. The first thing I did was get a journal and put it by my bedside. Then I wrote down the question that I wanted answered. I only wrote the first letter of each word, in case anyone decided to snoop in my journal. After I had written the question, I then laid down and took several deep breaths before falling off to sleep. The next morning—nothing. I laid there waiting for the answer. I knew enough not to move though, because I wanted to remember my dream. I knew I needed to be still and let it come to me. I laid there in complete silence and eventually, it came to me. I remembered my dream. When I remembered my dream, I got up and wrote it down. I continued doing this for about a week. After a week, I took my journal and looked for any patterns in the dreams. Sometimes I'd only remember symbols, still I wrote them down. I researched the internet for the meaning of my dreams.

There was one dream that I had during this time that I will never forget. It was a dream of a beloved woman from my childhood who had just passed. Her name was Isabelle. She was a lovely woman who was married to a man she adored. I can still remember the frequent laughter they shared with each other. Shortly before she appeared in my dream, I had attended her funeral service after she died suddenly. In the dream she gave me two keys. I looked at the keys, and one was for home, the other for work. I tried both of these keys in the door of her house. Neither of my keys worked. There was so much meaning in that dream that it would take months for me to get it. I knew the fact that my keys did not fit into a door that led to a happy home had some serious significance.

What I learned from that dream is that I had the keys to change my life, and that it was time to take the steps. My ability to interpret this dream really gave me the clarity and strength I needed to make the changes in my life. Before the dream, I was denying that I had any problems in my marriage. It was way too painful to accept the issues. I was also struggling with issues of self-esteem and co- dependency.

By continuing to analyze my dreams, I was able to get at what was really bugging me and then make corrections. The insights that come from dreams can take you to levels of personal awareness and clarity that you may not have thought possible. You will not regret looking into your dreams a little deeper. It's as if the mind turns into some type of super human problem solver while we sleep. Most of us wake up and get so busy with the mundane tasks of the day, that we can't hear what our dreams have discovered and are waiting to reveal.

The best way that I have learned to listen to the results of my dreams is to lie quietly in bed after I wake. I don't advise using an alarm clock, but waking naturally. Ease into the world so that your mind knows that it is okay to reveal itself. Slow your breathing, and be patient. Over time the practice will get easier, but don't expect perfection or consistency in terms of remembering your dreams. Just give gratitude for the days that you do remember your dreams.

Don't File For Divorce Just Yet

9

IS YOUR LIFE BETTER BECAUSE OF HIM?

If you are angry with your partner right now, you may not want to answer this question at this time. But, if you think about it—really think about it—it's simple. Does this man that you are with make your life better?

I'm not talking about how much you may love him or how great he is or even how much money he may have. But, simply ask yourself, on a day-to-day basis... does your man make your life easier and better? This question occurred to me after listening to a close friend who was trying to decide which suitor was right for her. She was fortunate to have several men who wanted to be with her, but she didn't know how to triage them, to put it lightly.

There was one guy who she loved desperately who was a tall, handsome, international traveler who loved her and wanted to be with her, but always seemed to have some personal difficulties. Then there was another man who she wasn't as attracted to, but did little things for her like getting her car repaired, calling to check on her, and other kind gestures. Listening to her, it occurred to me that at the end of the day, a real man is going to make your life easier, not more difficult. I also discovered that you will know who is right for you by the affect and impact he has on your life.

Take some time and write down all the ways that your partner makes your life easier for you.

1.

2.

3.

4.

5.

6.

7.

8.

9.

10.

Next, write down all the ways that you believe that your partner makes your life more difficult.

1.

2.

3.

4.

5.

6.

7.

8.

9.

10.

Now take a minute and review your answers. Do the good things he does outweigh the others? Sometimes the things we complain about really aren't that big in the scheme of things. The truth is we all are guilty of letting our partner's annoying habits outweigh the value that our partners bring to the relationship.

Don't File For Divorce Just Yet

10

PROS AND CONS

Some people say you shouldn't use pros and cons to make a decision about a relationship. I'd tend to agree if that was the sole method you used. Everyone knows it's not that cut and dried. With that said, there is some benefit to seeing things on paper. It helps to really lay out the issues and see how they shake out in the end. For me, a list of pros and cons helps me see if the pros really outweigh the cons or whether they are balanced. That at least gives me some guide as to whether my thinking is off or right on point.

Allow yourself to think back to when you were dating. Remember what it was that attracted you to your mate. A list of "Pros" can help you see what is working in your relationship, and help you determine whether it is enough to stay where you are. I am hopeful that the list will generate some very positive feelings about your mate. List anything that comes to mind, anything good that is, and get to writing.

PROS

1.

2.

3.

4.

Now it's time for the "cons." If you were really fair about your partner's positive attributes, then you should be feeling too good about him to possibly say anything bad about him that cannot be scientifically verified. So, when you are ready, make a list of the things about him that don't quite sit well with you. Start your list by listing the items that really get under your skin. Then add the small stuff.

CONS

1.

2.

3.

4.

What You Must Know First

We are not done yet. As I mentioned, a list of pros and cons by itself is not particularly helpful. So, take a look at the questions below, and answer each question as it relates to your partner.

1. Do you like him as a person?
2. Would you select him as a friend?
3. Does he make you happy 51% of the time?
4. Do his actions result in you crying frequently?
5. Do you like the way he smells?
6. Do you laugh together?
7. Can you confide in him?
8. Are you comfortable being vulnerable with him?
9. Does he humiliate you in front of others?
10. Has your self-esteem suffered as a result of the relationship?
11. Is he good with the children?
12. Is he jealous?
13. Is he frequently depressed or angry?
14. Do you get wet when you think about him?
15. How do you feel when you think about him being with someone else?
16. If he never changed, could you spend the rest of your life with him?
17. Are you in love with him?
18. Do you love him?
19. Are you completely comfortable naked with him?

20. Can you tell him what you want sexually?
21. Does he listen to you?
22. Is he the first person you would call if you got a big promotion?

PROS AND CONS

Now that you have addressed the pros and cons and answered the questions, take a look at your answers.

Try spending an hour writing your thoughts about each of the pros, cons, and your answers to the questions. Expect a few tears and laughs. I'd recommend the writing portion of this exercise be completed over the course of a few days. Really get at the issues and what your true feelings are about the issues.

The act of writing can help to center your thoughts. Just the process will force you to get clear about whether you need to stay and work on your relationship, or whether it is in your best interest to move on.

Here's an exercise to help you wake up and see what role you are playing in your marriage. This will enable you to be in a better position to decide whether to stay or go. Please write your answers in your journal.

1. Identify 1 to 3 serious issues that you believe are causing your marital difficulties.

2. Look back at each of those incidents and describe the events that led up to the incidents in detail. Describe who was there when it happened, how many times it happened, and where it happened.

3. Describe your thoughts and feelings at the time it happened. What were you thinking? Did you have any physical sensations?

4. Describe what, if any, actions you took before, during, or after the event occurred.

5. Write down any and all words that the two of you said to each other, as well as any words that others might have spoken.

6. Write down any advice you received from your mother, clergy, or friends about the incident.

After you complete this exercise in your journal, wait a few days and then take a look at what you have written. Take some time to write down any patterns you see in how you responded to the problem or situation that you believe your spouse caused.

Next, write a page or two to describe how you might have responded differently, and the ideal response you expected from your spouse.

This exercise will give you a tremendous insight into what role you play in your marital issues. It will also give you insight into what you expect from your spouse. This in turn will help you to decide whether you can fix your marriage by fixing something about yourself, although I am sure you are perfect. The exercise can also help you by examining your expectations. Are they realistic, or are they unrealistic given your personality and that of your mate?

11

IS THAT US?

It's easier to see ourselves in other people. That's why movies are so popular. They allow us to see ourselves in real-time, on the big screen. One of my favorite movies is A Beautiful Mind. I love that movie because we get to see, through John Nash's eyes, that our thoughts can fool us. In the movie, Russell Crowe plays John Nash, a brilliant mathematician plagued by schizophrenia. In the beginning of the movie, John Nash is called by the Pentagon to decipher mathematical codes and thwart an impending Soviet plot. The movie goers see all the characters that are actually products of Mr. Nash's mental illness, but that doesn't stop the movie goers. Like him, we really believe that somebody is after John Nash. We are right there with him. We see the Pentagon officials in the situation room who are plotting with him.

Wow! I thought what I believed was true, because, well, I thought it… You get the point. A Beautiful Mind was a skillful lesson in how important it is to question your thoughts. The same is true for relationships. We can't always see ourselves, and when we do, what we see is only our perception, and maybe our perception is not the exact truth. I think the best we can do is to try to see ourselves objectively, and then make decisions based on a clear picture.

Get your tea and take a look at the couples in the next exercises. The scenarios mentioned below can help you open your eyes to some of the hidden, or obvious, issues you may see in your own relationship.

BETH AND RICH

Beth met Rich while she was in high school. He was the football quarterback and she was head of the school newspaper. He was exceptionally good looking, but was not aware of his looks. They appeared to be opposites, but they got along great. They shared the same interests, respected each other, and genuinely loved one another. They married soon after college. Theirs was a great relationship for ten years until Rich began having an affair with a woman at work. Beth found out when she heard them having telephone sex. It turns out that he and the woman, Ashley, had been dating for a year and Ashley was now four months pregnant with Rich's first son. Beth was distraught. She wanted to know why. Rich couldn't answer why; all he knew was that he really wanted to be with Beth. He admitted that he had thought he was in love with Ashley, but he really wanted Beth. Beth had no idea what to do. She cried and cried for months, but eventually took Rich back. They went to counseling together for several months. Ashley had the baby and Rich stayed with Beth. Rich and Beth are still together. Rich has remained faithful.

Do you think Beth should have taken Rich back? Could you have taken him back? Could you have ever trusted Rich again?

ELLEN AND JEFF

Ellen and Jeff met at work. He was her manager when they started dating.

They dated for two years and eventually married. Other than work, Ellen and Jeff really had no common interests. They were, however, drawn together by Ellen's magnetic personality. Eventually, they had children together. Once the children came, they began to have difficulties. They both worked, but Ellen had the bulk of the childcare responsibilities. Jeff did very little around the house and Ellen felt put upon. He'd come home and put his feet up while she took care of everything. Eventually, Ellen's magnetic personality began to change because Jeff acted a little too lazily around the house. Jeff refused to get a maid, saying they couldn't afford it. Eventually, Ellen began to look haggard from work, the kids, and lack of sleep. She stopped going out with her friends and did little to take care of herself. She began to gain weight and look frumpy. The two of them never went anywhere together. Jeff looked great because when he wasn't working he was either sleeping or playing ball with his boys. Ellen insisted they go to counseling several times, but Jeff refused. Ellen began to drink to deal with the issues in her relationship.

What do you think Ellen might do to improve her situation? What is Jeff saying to Ellen if he won't work on their relationship? Does this scenario even remotely resemble your relationship? If so, how much on a scale of one to ten?

CAMILLE AND TONY

Camille and Tony met at a Maxwell concert. It was love at first sight. They got along great, and were married in less than a year. Camille and Tony were lucky. They had many of the same interests, respected each other, and had great communication. There was just this one issue: they had different sex drives. Camille loved to have sex. Tony could more or less do without it. In the early years of their marriage this wasn't so much of a problem, that is until Camille hit her mid-forties and her sex drive hit the roof. She talked with Tony about her desires. He was not interested in hearing about sex. He said at their age, sex just wasn't that important and that it was overrated. After much pushing, Tony agreed to go to counseling with her. They learned lots of new things together, which improved their sex lives together. Unfortunately, after several months, Tony fell back into his old habit of denying Camille sex. Camille was distraught. It wasn't long before she began smiling back at Jake, a slightly younger man at her job. Soon Jake and Camille began having an affair. Today, Camille and Tony are still married. Camille is still seeing Jake on a regular basis and believes she is in love with him. Tony is not aware of the affair, but his relationship with Camille has improved because they no longer bicker over sex.

Do you think Camille was wrong? Do you think she should have suffered in silence? What might she have done to improve her situation? Does this scenario even remotely resemble your relationship?

KATE AND JOSH

Kate met Josh in accounting class. He earned an A and she received a D. When they married, Josh, an accountant, used this as a reason that he should manage the money. Kate gave in because she didn't work and Josh did. Kate was a stay-at-home mom. Josh controlled all of the money and gave Kate an allowance. When Kate tried to get a job, Josh threatened to leave her and take the kids. Kate had a college degree, but no work experience outside the home. As they grew older, Josh became even more controlling about money issues. He eventually stopped giving her any allowance. She began borrowing from friends and family members for clothes for her and the children. Josh refused to go to counseling with her. He insisted he did not have a problem with money. He often berated her lack of money knowledge and frequently called her stupid whenever they discussed money.

What do you think Kate should do? Is there anything she should do to improve the relationship? Does this scenario even remotely resemble your relationship?

CASEY AND ANTHONY

Casey came from a very poor background and grew up in a trailer park. She was attractive with curly brown shoulder-length hair and an hourglass figure. Her dream was to marry a doctor, live in a large house, drive a Mercedes, and have a closet filled with designer clothes. Casey got her dream when she met Anthony while she was in nursing school. Anthony was a well-established doctor in the small community where Casey went to nursing school. He was not as handsome as the men she was used to dating, but he was nice enough, and he was financially secure. So when he asked her to go out with him, she jumped at the chance. They dated for two months before Anthony proposed to Casey. Casey said yes, but she was not physically attracted to him and they were not compatible on many different levels. Still she said yes because Anthony represented financial security and the chance at a family life Casey had dreamed about. The problem was she did not love Anthony for

Anthony. In fact, she really did not know him.

Their marriage worked until their children grew to an age where they did not need Casey as much. Without her children to focus on, Casey was left with the reality that she did not love her husband. The Mercedes, the designer clothes, and sprawling mansion were not enough to keep her chained in a loveless marriage. Casey began to withhold sex from him, angry that she was stuck with a man she did not want to be with. The money and status he provided ultimately were not enough for Casey. She began to feel repulsed by Anthony. Sadly, Anthony sensed it and began drinking, staying out late, and eventually he had an affair with Casey's best friend, Mia. Once Anthony had the affair, Casey was free to leave him and then blame him for the dissolution of their marriage.

What do you think Casey could have done different? Was her loveless marriage to Anthony worth saving? Does this scenario even remotely resemble your relationship? If so, how?

ANGELA AND ETHAN

Angela married Ethan right out of college. She was in love with him from the day they met. Ethan loved her back, but cheated on her twice in the two years before they were married. Still Angela married him, believing that her love for Ethan would be more than enough to carry them through. The years went by and they had three beautiful little girls. From the outside looking in, it appeared as though they were happy. They both had great jobs, a house in the suburbs, and children that they adored.

It was about six years into their marriage that Angela began to drink. She began drinking because she felt lonely since Ethan was never home and was rumored to have another family across town.

Ethan was a serial cheater who would bring his mistress on family vacations. Angela's response was drinking. It started with a glass of wine once a week, then two glasses every day, until she began drinking a bottle of wine each night, while her family slept soundly. Angela was determined to stay with Ethan, and she did. She stayed with him so long that she died from the cirrhosis of the liver from drinking away the pain she felt from his lack of affection.

What do you think Angela might have done differently? Was her loveless marriage to Anthony worth saving? Does this scenario even remotely resemble your relationship? If so, how?

Don't File For Divorce Just Yet

12

VIOLENT COMMUNICATION

When I was sixteen years old, I had a boyfriend named Keith who was abusive. I was madly in love with him when he hit me the first time. He swore it wouldn't happen again, but it did happen again, again, and again. Once he knocked me down and tried to drag me across the asphalt on the playground. Then another time he came to the apartment I lived in with my mother and younger sister. I was the only one at home. He was banging on the door with a crazed look in his eyes yelling for me to open the door. For some reason I told him no. I refused to open the door. I peeked out the peek hole to see him brandishing a serrated knife yelling at me. I don't recall being scared, that was until he kicked the door in and came chasing after me. I ran through the small apartment and hid behind a small wooden end table. He came at me. I grabbed a lamp. Just then I looked up and saw a blond haired woman and two gentlemen coming through the space where the front door had been. I was embarrassed to be standing there with a lamp in my hand, but truly relieved to see these strangers. It turns out they were from the Jehovah's Witness group and they were going door to door. What were the chances of that? If I ever questioned God, that was my reminder.

A few weeks after the door incident, I was sitting in my 10th grade Spanish Class. I remember it being a beautiful spring day and I had driven my mother's car to school. Just seeing his face I felt tense, embarrassed, and scared. By the grace of God, my Spanish teacher recognized this and he would not let Keith in the class room. Keith tried to push his way in and the teacher called the front office. Keith was escorted from the building, but insisted on waiting for me in the parking lot. By the time I reached the parking lot, there were local police cars everywhere to escort me to my car. I have no idea why the cars were there, and I still don't know. All I know is that I experienced a brief sense of safety.

I remember getting in my car and driving home. I felt relieved as I drove through the wooded area on the way home from my high school to my grandmother's house. I wasn't far from home when I stopped at a stop light. My window was down. It was spring and the music was playing. The next thing I know it was Keith. He reached into the car, grabbed my necklace in an effort to strangle me. I pulled away as best I could. People were all around me. Joggers. Other cars. Still no one, not a soul stopped to help. Then Keith punched me in the face through the window. At that point I hit the gas and took off through a red light. I was in pain—astonished at all the people passing by who just kept passing. The ability to ignore human suffering is another book. I will only say that I've learned that bravery takes courage, and we are all in various stages of development on that one. This I know for sure.

Anyway, I went home after the school incident that day, and told my mother what happened. We immediately went to the local magistrate to get a peace bond. However, somehow Keith and his mother found us. His mother assured my mother that he would not do it again. And you know what? He did not. He never bothered me again, not once. His next girlfriend, may God rest her soul, was not so lucky. He was convicted of shooting her three times point blank in the chest. She died, leaving a small town divided and a toddler with no mother.

Keith received a life sentence.

When I started this book, I did not expect to bare my soul on my own personal experience with violence. That topic still brings issues of fear, shame, and embarrassment for me. So, my first drafts of this book glossed over the issue. That is until one night, I began researching the topic of violence and women for this book. It was then that I knew I had to tell my own story, for my own sake, as well as that of the readers. I had to tell it because God spared my life. I know that I am one of the lucky ones. This I know for sure.

If you have been hit, even once, I encourage

you to contact the National Domestic Violence Hotline at 1-800-799-7233, and if it happens again please call 911 immediately. Statistics say that 1.3 million each year are the victims of physical assault by an intimate partner. Too many of these victims wind up dead at the hands of their boyfriends or husbands. I'd like to believe that their deaths might have been prevented if the women walked out at the first signs of abuse, whether it started with physical, financial, or emotional abuse.

So please, if you have been physically assaulted by your boyfriend or lover, please contact the National Domestic Violence Hotline. The Hotline is a nonprofit organization that provides crisis intervention, information, and referral to victims of domestic violence or their friends.

The National Coalition Against Domestic Violence advocates creating a Safety Plan. I encourage you to visit their web site to learn more about creating a safety plan for yourself if you are in a physically abusive relationship. The website address is: www.ncadv.org. The most important thing about the safety list is that it can help keep you safe.

I know it may be difficult to tell anyone that you are in a physically abusive relationship, because then the question becomes, why don't you get out? Unfortunately, it's not always that easy. Still, it's important to tell at least one person. If you can't do it for yourself, do it for your children, grandchildren, nieces, or nephews. Your children need you, so please tell at least one person and develop a code word for when they should help.

NCADV also has excellent tips for women who have left a relationship. I strongly recommend visiting this website whether you are in an abusive relationship, or whether you have recently decided to end an abusive relationship.

EMOTIONAL ABUSE

Emotional abuse is more difficult to uncover because it can be subtle, but it is a serious problem because emotional abuse often escalates into physical abuse when subtle techniques no longer work on the victim. Even worse, abusers will often resort to physical abuse of your children if their emotional abuse no longer works on you. Here are some areas to keep an eye on, and remember if you are unsure you are being abused, you can always contact the Domestic Violence Hotline.

INTIMIDATION

- Does he make you afraid by giving you nasty looks, or making threatening gestures?
- Does he smash things when he's angry at you?
- Does he destroy your property?
- Does he display weapons to threaten you?

- Does he threaten to hurt you?

- Does he threaten to leave you?

- Does he threaten to commit suicide if you do not do what he wants?
- Does he treat you like a servant and he's the master?

- Does he stalk you?

- Do you feel like you are walking on egg shells around your boyfriend or spouse?

USING ISOLATION

- Does he try to control where you go?

- Does he try to control what you say or do?

- Does he justify his control by calling it jealousy?

- Does he berate most of your friends?

- Does he find reasons why you shouldn't associate with certain friends/ family members?

USING CHILDREN

- Does he threaten to take the children away?

- Does he use the children to relay messages?
- Does he talk bad about you to the children?
- Does he constantly denigrate your parenting skills?

MINIMIZING, DENYING AND BLAMING

- Does he say everything is your fault?
- Does he blame you for every problem in your relationship?

FINANCIAL ABUSE

- Does he control all of the monetary decisions?
- Does he make you ask for money?
- Does he refuse to give you access to family finances?
- Does he refuse to allow you to get or keep a job?

For more information, I encourage you to visit the following websites:
http://www.domesticviolence.org
http://www.ncadv.org

Don't File For Divorce Just Yet

13

TRIAL SEPARATION

Every time I look at the heading for this chapter, it scares me because it requires real action, and represents the unknown. Although this option may invoke fear, it is an option for deciding whether you will stay or go.

Once you get past the fear, a trial separation is actually a good tool if you use it properly. On the other hand, your particular issues may not be suited for a trial separation. You may need to leave sooner if your spouse is physically abusing you or your children. Either way, speaking with a counselor before is always wise before embarking on a trial separation. Professional counselors can be helpful in that they are an objective third party who may help you see issues that you were previously unaware of.

After you've spoken with a counselor, you might consider getting your spouse to attend counseling with you. For some men this is no easy feat. However, I can tell you the one time that a man will really attend counseling is when he's faced with the choice of his wife leaving him. If he refuses to go to counseling, even when faced with divorce, then you pretty much have your answer about how much he is willing to work on your marriage and on himself.

If he agrees to go to counseling then you and the counselor can raise the idea of trial separation, or you can do it on your own. It just really depends on how open the lines of communication are between you and your spouse. Sometimes a neutral third party can really work wonders, particularly when you are entering unchartered waters as with a trial separation.

Once both you and your spouse agree to the trial separation, you can work with your therapist on the details. A trial separation can be great because it can really help you see whether you want to live on your own or whether you want to return to your family. Yes, it's a risk that your spouse may not want to return to the marriage. There is always that possibility.

As scary as it is, there is also the possibility that you may love living on your own—although, it is hard to believe when you have been in the cocoon of marriage for a long time. I found a tremendous amount of peace in singlehood. Oh, I miss my children terribly when they are spending time with their father, but the time has allowed me to get back to the business of being me. I recently had brunch with a favorite cousin who said that I was my old self, and that I was filled with life. You have no idea how good that made me feel. I knew my marriage had sucked the life out of me. I had let it. But boy did it feel good to know that I was my old self again, and that it was so obvious that others could see it.

Then there is the possibility that you may not like living on your own. Make no mistake, it is tough living on your own; it was for me, in the beginning anyway. You already know about my snow mishaps. There was also the incident of the three clogged bathrooms in my new home. I bought three different plungers before I could figure out how to free all that toilet paper my sons had stuffed into the toilets. My first husband had always unclogged the toilets. There was also the time I put my own windshield wiper fluid in my car. I had rarely lifted the hood of my car in my first marriage. These are small things, but I felt like I had climbed Mount Everest after I completed them for the first time on my own.

Then there's the issue of just having a man in the house. That was difficult for me at first. Not having my husband around was rough, no matter how bad things were between us. Sometimes the loneliness was unbearable, despite all the friends I had surrounding me. Fortunately I figured out that alone does not mean lonely, and it was not long before I was cherishing my alone time.

Regarding your children, it is important that you keep their routine the same as much as possible. My children's father and I both live within minutes of each other so that we can co-parent and so the children can remain in the same school district. This familiarity was important for the children as much as it was for their dad and me. Seeing familiar things helped to ground us all while we are experiencing the separation. It is also very important to consult with a child psychiatrist before discussing separation with your children. I'd strongly recommend counseling for the children during this time. Even if you don't see them reacting, they are like sponges and will soak up all the tension and chaos that may be going on between you and your spouse. So as their mother, please make sure that counseling is high on the list. I can also speak from personal experience. I remember when my parents split. I felt tremendous pain and acted out by earning an F in gym. Yes, I can say it now. I failed gym. How? I was defiant and would not change my clothes and get sweaty because I'd spent way too much time getting dressed for the day to mess up my makeup in a gym class… It's funny now, but that was my reasoning. So, please for me, at least have the kids talk with a school guidance counselor.

Here are some major areas to consider before opting for a trial separation:

1. Set the ground rules
   Start drawing up the perfect scenario for you, and then go back and consider what objections your spouse may have. You can then make any adjustments you feel may be warranted.
2. Living arrangements
   Who will stay at the house? Who will move out? Will you both rent your current home, and then get separate apartments?

3. Finances
   This is a great time to begin handling your own finances if you have not done so before. You might consider opening individual accounts if you don't already have them. Consider using one joint account for any joint expenses that will continue.
4. Lawyers
   Do not put anything down on paper until you have discussed your plan with a lawyer. You have no idea how men can change if and when you actually decide to leave. You do not want to put anything in writing, with your signature, that you have not first cleared with a lawyer. You can get a free consult, initially, by calling around to different lawyers. We love to talk and we have big egos, so please pick up the phone, because we actually like to help people with their problems.

Be as clear about the following issues as you can, allowing for much needed flexibility:

- Will you both date other people during the separation?

- Will you continue to meet with a therapist?

I'd also strongly recommend starting a diary the month prior to your move. Write down what you are feeling, what the issues are, and why you believe a separation is needed. Then continue to keep the diary during the entire separation. This will give you a record to look at to help you decide whether you are really ready to go back to your spouse and try again, or whether you and your children will be happier on your own.

PART II QUICK TIPS

- Evaluate yourself and the role you play in your relationship difficulties.
- Weigh the pros and cons of staying versus going.

- Consider and explore a trial separation.

- Visit www.ncadv.org if you suspect your relationship is emotionally or physically abusive.

PART III

STAYING

WITH ALL HIS QUIRKS AND IMPERFECTIONS—HE IS YOURS!

Don't File For Divorce Just Yet

STAYING

Fifteen years. That's how long I was married. Does that mean my relationship was a failure? Quite the contrary. As far as relationships go, it was very successful—until it wasn't. Still, if I knew the things that I learned when researching for this book, I can say that the quality of my relationship would have been better and possibly the duration of my relationship would have been longer. My hope is that you can benefit from what I learned.

One big discovery for me was that everyone argues about the same stuff: Sex, Money, Communication and Sex, Money and Communication. Even if you were married to the hottest, sexiest, kindest, richest stud in the world, chances are you'd disagree on the same issues; sex, money, and communication. The reason is that he is not you. What matters is not that you disagree, but how you disagree about sex, money, and communication.

Don't File For Divorce Just Yet

14

MONEY

If I had to pinpoint the main issues in my marriage, I would have to say it was money, money, and more money. Big surprise there. Most couples struggle with money at some point. The trick is not to let it destroy your relationship. Our own attitudes and beliefs about money undid us.

Like most couples, we came from different backgrounds, with different beliefs and attitudes about money. I was very naïve when I married. I thought that we would only argue if we did not have enough money. Don't get me wrong, we were not rich, but our biggest disagreements were about how we would spend the money we did have. Looking back, there never seemed to be enough money to do the things I thought were important like buying furniture and taking vacations. I wasn't asking for anything extravagant, but for some reason it took us 10 years to get decent furniture and we took one vacation for pleasure without the children in 14 years of marriage. Furniture and vacations are important to me, especially vacations.

I come from a traveling family. It's in our blood. I remember hearing stories about an uncle who would walk from Media, Pennsylvania to Richmond, Virginia every spring. Then there were the cross-country trips that my mother took my sister and me on. She did all this with her very close friend Francis, Francis' granddaughter, a tremendous sense of adventure, and a book called Mexico on $5 a Day. I still remember us packing up that old Nova and driving across the U.S.—all the way from Media, PA to Saltillo, Mexico in 1975.

That thirst for travel has never left me. I also knew you did not need a lot of money to travel. So for me not to travel, somewhere, anywhere, was unnatural and caused a lot of internal strife within me and inside my marriage. I am happy to say that in the year after we separated, I traveled to Missouri, New Orleans, Atlanta, and Florida. My mother and I also took my boys on their first plane ride to Disney World.

Looking back, our issue with vacations was not at all about money, because we could have saved money to take a vacation. Instead, the issue was our different beliefs about spending money on a vacation.

In her book, *Money, Sex, and Kids*, Tina B. Tessina, Ph.D., talks about the value of understanding your own attitudes about money, as well as how to talk about money. The author reminds us that our attitudes about money generally stem from the role that money played in our family when we were growing up.

The attitudes you or your mate may have will likely involve issues surrounding scarcity, love and approval, status and power. For me, travel is about bonding with family. That trip to Mexico was one of the few times during my youth that I had my mother to myself. Also, when we traveled as a family, it was usually to visit other family members. So, yes, money spent on travel and vacation was money well spent in my view.

How my family spent money also sent a powerful message because while we did not have a lot of money growing up, the fact that a portion of it was allocated for travel said a whole lot about what we valued and what was important.

SCARCITY

If your family did not have enough money to pay for food, clothing or shelter when you were growing up, you may have developed certain fears and anxieties about money. This is not a bad thing. Some money fears can lead you to become an excellent money manager who creates a perfect balance between spending and saving. That wasn't the case for me. I recall that we had more than most people in the small community where I grew up; still, I can recall my father saying that he was always broke. This was a powerful statement because it made me believe that as a kid I was broke too. So inside I felt like we were poor and money was scarce. It didn't help that I lived outside a wealthy suburb called Wallingford in Pennsylvania where my grandmother cleaned houses for the wealthy residents, as did many other women in the community. My grandfather picked up their trash. There's just something about that fact that made me feel as though I was poor, despite how comfortably my family lived.

Also, I was raised by a single mother for most of my life. So that fact in itself led me to believe that we just didn't have enough money. Whether it was true or not, these were the factors at play in my mind. Now do you think my distorted views about scarcity shaped my belief about money? You bet! Unfortunately, all my fears about money went back to the fear that I would never have enough and my mistaken belief that I was somehow not as good as other people who had more money than me or my family.

I'm not alone in these fears. So if money was scarce or you simply believed it was scarce, then do the exercise below. If scarcity was clearly not your issue, then explore this issue as it may relate to your spouse. You might complete the exercise below based on what you know about your spouse. At a minimum, this will give you some insight into how and what he may be feeling as it relates to money.

1. Describe why you believed your family did not have enough money during childhood.
2. Describe how you felt as a child regarding your family's lack of money. Why?

3. Do you get a headache at the thought of spending money?
4. Do you fear that you will run out of money and wind up homeless?
5. Identify three ways that money scarcity currently impacts the way you spend or save money.
6. Describe any money issues you have with your mate and see how your own attitudes related to money scarcity may be at play.

LOVE AND APPROVAL

Despite my perceived money scarcity, we had enough money in my family to use money for love and approval. In our family, money was used to show love. I can still remember my grandfather giving me a dollar almost every time he walked through the door, or my grandmother slipping me a rolled-up dollar bill or my mother giving me money to go to the mall.

These were small but very important acts of love and I am grateful for the love they showed me, make no mistake. I hold none of them responsible for what I learned from how they showed me love. I know I am lucky to have been so loved. Still the messages carried over into how I raised my own kids, and at one point I can remember my first husband and I spending $300 a month on our sons at Toys R Us. That's right, any old month my sons were making out like bandits because we loved them so much!

It wasn't until I took a look at our budget that I realized the pattern. We had no choice but to stop. Not only could we not afford to spend the money, there was no need to do this. It's funny when we quit spending all that money, our kids automatically adjusted because they had so much stuff to play with already. It also got easier, in time, for us to tell them no, we cannot afford a certain video game.

The end result is that now the boys are very good about handling their own money and they fully understand that we only give gifts on birthdays and during the holidays. Now, they only ask for a few things at Christmas, always keeping in mind the value and cost of what they are asking for.

If money was used to show love and approval when you or your spouse were growing up, take a minute to complete the exercise below.

1. How was money used to show love or approval in your family?
2. Describe how you felt as a child regarding your family's lack of money.
3. Do you get a headache at the thought of spending money?
4. Do you fear that you will run out of money and wind up homeless?
5. Identify three ways that money scarcity currently impacts the way you spend or save money.

6. Describe any money issues you have with your mate and see how your own attitudes related to money scarcity may be at play.

STATUS

Spending money on status should be pretty easy to spot. In my case, it meant that I wanted to have a bigger house than everyone. Oh, I got the house—it was a 7,000 square foot French provincial-style home with 17 rooms and 48 windows. We purchased the house for a steal in 1998, because the real estate market was down in our area and the owner was eager to sell the property for personal reasons. When she met us, she said we were a nice couple and she lowered the price by $50,000. All I could think was that this house was meant for us.

I can still remember my sister-in-law asking how I intended to clean that house. It's hilarious now, but I hadn't even thought about cleaning that house. I was 32-years-old at the time and all I could think about was the status I would have in owning the home. What she probably should have asked me was how I intended to pay for the home, particularly once I had my sons and could not bear to leave them to go to a job. No, I didn't see that coming either—the fact that I would love my kids so much that it didn't matter where I lived, only that they were happy and healthy. Nor did I see the debt we'd run up in refinancing the house, or the huge oil bills that would follow. Ah, love truly is blind.

Nor was it a coincidence that I had to have that Jaguar. A big old white one. I had it for three years until I crashed it. Just like that, the car was gone, crumpled in the front like a damn accordion. The image still haunts me. For days I cried over my car, not really appreciating the fact I survived a serious accident with nothing more than a one-inch bruise on my collar bone. I was on my way to my mother's 70th birthday party, and all my cousins were in the cars behind me. My sons had gone ahead with my mother fortunately. It would be a long time before I really appreciated how lucky I was that day, not just to have survived the crash, but that my children weren't in the car with me. When I crashed, I had about 10 relatives there to help me because they were all headed to my mother's birthday party. Looking back, that was my "a-ha moment." The family surrounding me was there. The car was gone, but I had what was most important. Fortunately, I received a second chance to really learn about what is important in this life…and not a day goes by that I don't give thanks.

Take a minute to do the next exercise, whether or not you believe status is an issue for yourself or your mate. The reality is that we live in America, and with all the commercials about the rich and famous, it's very likely that status issues have crept into your family one way or another.

1. Describe the facts about why you believe money was used to gain status in your family.
2. Describe how you felt as a child regarding your family's status in the community.
3. Recall a time when you wanted a toy and your parents said you couldn't afford it. How did you feel?
4. What about now? Do you have a large home you have trouble affording, or other trappings of success that may be causing money problems?
5. Identify three ways that your need for status may have impacted a recent purchase.
6. Describe any money issues you have with your mate and see how your own need for status may be at play.

One last word about status—we all need status in one way or another, but there are other ways to get it besides spending money. For me, it meant serving as PTA President at my children's school. Yes, this was a lot of work, but it satisfied my need to be head honcho without costing me a dime. By satisfying your need for status in non-monetary ways, you can save a ton of money and hopefully improve your relationship in the meantime.

GUIDELINES FOR DISCUSSING MONEY

Aside from attitudes about money, there's always the issue of discussing money. Sometimes couples can't even discuss the subject, which can lead to marital and financial doom. I'm hoping this is not the case for you, but if it is, not to worry. Here are some good tips to get talking about money based on information in Money, Sex, and Kids.

1. Share your different attitudes about money.
   You can do this by using what you may have learned from this book regarding your own attitudes about money. Also, you should be in a better position to understand your mate's attitude about money, once you've examined how a deeply-held belief can shape how we spend money. Armed with new information, it's also very likely that you will be more understanding about money decisions your mate may have made, which will make it easier to see his point of view on money issues.
2. Discuss Financial Goals.
   You might want to take some time to examine what your own goals are before discussing them with your mate. Shared goals can really help a marriage move along.

Here are some areas that you and your spouse might discuss:

- Savings: How much do you want and need for short-term and long-term savings?
- College funds: When do you plan to start saving, and how much can you afford to save?
- Retirement: How do you want to spend your life after you retire?
- Other Assets: Do you want to buy a larger house, or a new car? Do you want to purchase a summer home or timeshare?
- Vacations: Where do you want to go for vacation this year, or in five years?

You might get started on these areas and then come up with other areas to discuss. In any case, I'd recommend writing down your goals and keeping them in an obvious place. This will keep you both focused, give you something to look forward to, and serve as a reminder of how well you two can work together!

If you can work on your attitude about money and learn to talk about money, then you are on your way to creating and maintaining a healthier relationship.

# Don't File For Divorce Just Yet

15

SEX

A very close friend recently confided in me that she makes love to her husband at least four times a week, every week, and more if he wants it. She is close to fifty and her sex drive is lagging. She does not always want to make love to him. Still she puts on her Victoria Secret nightgown, smiles and they make love. Why? Because she understands how to keep her husband happy. She also understands the reality that if she is not satisfying his desires, she is leaving it open for someone else to do her job.

Sex can be a big issue in marriages. It always seems like someone wants it too much and the other person doesn't want it enough. Couples aren't always sexually compatible, which is an unfortunate fact of life. Some people like chocolate cake, some like carrot cake, so why would our preferences in the bedroom be any different?

The first step to satisfying sex is knowing how to please yourself. Be sure to experiment; you may start out with your own hands and then graduate to a vibrator, but whatever it is, just make sure you know how to please you. You have no idea how much stress knowing how to please yourself can relieve.

This will go a long way if you have a partner with a low sexual libido, or if you have an unusually high sexual drive. There is nothing wrong with either scenario, you just have to know how to handle it so that it does not become a problem in your marriage.

After you are comfortable pleasing yourself, and if this applies to you, consider becoming more sexually assertive. This way you are assured to get what you want in the bedroom. You have no idea how many issues knock 'em down, drag 'em out sex can fix…

In their book, The Assertive Woman, Stanlee Phelps and Nancy Austin developed something called a Personal Sensuality Survey. They encourage knowing yourself: know what you like and don't like, know what makes you have an orgasm. They also encourage expressing yourself. Don't be afraid to ask for what you want, no matter how silly it may seem or embarrassed you may be. Knowing and expressing yourself is part of being a grown woman, and you'd be surprised at how your sexual assertiveness may turn your partner on. Also, this will free you from a passive, solely responsive sex life, if that is your issue.

What You Must Know First

Please take this Personal Sensuality Survey. It may give you a better sense of yourself in the love-making department.

1. How do you feel about making sounds or talking during lovemaking?
2. Are there any taboo words that you wouldn't dare utter to your lover during lovemaking?
3. Do you feel guilty when you masturbate?

4. Would you ever consider watching your lover masturbate?
5. Do you always expect the same level of orgasmic response?
6. How do you handle your sexual attraction towards others?
7. How do you communicate to your lover what you need in your lovemaking?
8. Do you have fantasies that you would like to act out?
9. How do you share these fantasies with your partner?
10. Do you ever initiate lovemaking?

11. Have you ever studied how to please a man sexually?

When you are done, review your answers. Is there anything on the list that you are willing to try?

Another idea, which I highly recommend, is "sexting." Sexting is sending a racy text message.

Don't be afraid to send your spouse a racy text message. If you don't text, then send an email. There's something very sexy about receiving a racy note. It seems to get all your senses involved, and really kick up the sexual anticipation that can sometimes fade in long-term relationships. If you don't know what to say, just say, "Hey, sexy…" That's enough to at least get the juices going and let your man know you still think he's hot!

Please "sext" responsibly! Never, ever "sext" using work computers or mobile device. Your information is not private, as you already know.

16

THE LITTLE THINGS

Inevitably it's the little things—they start out like rain drops, then transform into a torrential storm wreaking havoc on your marriage. Yes, the little things. I can remember my 10th grade English teacher saying her husband's failure to put the top on the toothpaste ultimately led to the demise of their marriage. So many things bother us for different reasons. It's something different for each of us. Maybe it's hearing your husband talk about football, cars, or even his job. Maybe it's that old belt he always wears. With love and understanding, you really can surmount these issues; because after all, in the scheme of things, they really are little things!

In their book *In Control*, Redford Williams, MD and Virginia Williams, Ph.D. discuss a simple three-step plan that you can use to get at the little things before they get at you.

Step 1: Describe the situation causing you negative thoughts and or feelings.
Step 2: Describe your feelings—calmly.
Step 3: Let him know what you want—gently.

Step 4: Acknowledge the difficulty your man may have complying with your request.

Be careful on this one. Make sure you don't come off condescending. You may even want to run this one by a friend or two. Do not, and I repeat, DO NOT attempt to discuss your relationship troubles with a man-hating, recently divorced, girlfriend because you won't get a good read.

17

YOUR MAN AND HIS EMOTIONS

As women, we have constant reminders of our own emotions, either through ourselves, through our girlfriends, on television, or in magazines. The images of emotional women are everywhere. But what of men? Yes, they have emotions, and not just anger. They just don't show their emotions the way we do. That concept was always difficult for me to grasp—maybe because I didn't have any brothers; which often times made me feel that I was a bit lacking in my understanding of men. I get it now though.

Men show emotions, just not in the manner that women do. Just because we can't see what they are feeling doesn't mean that they aren't feeling it. In practice, this is tricky; it's easy to overlook someone's feelings if they are not on display. I know that I am guilty of this. As women, it is easy for us to get so engrossed in caring for our children, handling family finances, and working that we can often miss the emotional cues that our men send us. Men don't generally cry and spill their hearts out, but if you have one that does, consider yourself lucky; you will always know what and how he feels.

For the rest of us, I'd recommend taking your man's emotional temperature every week or so. How do you do this? By remembering that men need to be trusted, appreciated, respected, and encouraged. Nothing complicated required here—just sit back in your easy chair with a cup of tea and think about him or watch him in loving silence. Has he been acting out of sorts? Is he unusually quiet, talkative, or demonstrating anything that is out of character? Has he been working late or hanging out too late? Has he been drinking too much? By observing his cues, you can learn a lot about what he is feeling, which can bring you closer to one another.

Once you know what he's feeling, you can offer up enough love, patience, and understanding to encourage him to express himself when the time is right. This doesn't mean pressuring him to talk. We all know that does not work. What works? Try this: whatever the issue is, raise it in bed, preferably after you have given him a blow job! Yes, I said it. Laugh or call me vulgar, but if you want to get at the issue you'll take my advice. If he doesn't open up while you're laying there after making love, he will in a few days. Just be patient and listen with kindness and love when he does open up. Practice patient laid-back silence, which can bring the hardest man out of his shell.

18

ACCEPTING WHAT IS

Sometimes no matter what you do, a situation does not improve to the extent that you may like. That is true with anything, like my weight. It took me a long time to accept being a size 14, but I learned to love myself, just as I am. This is a powerful feeling because without the stress of trying to lose weight, I am actually exercising and eating healthier. The result is that I feel and look better than I have in years, all because I practiced accepting me for me.

Accepting anything, whether it's weight or the fact that your spouse will never change, can be a hard pill to swallow. If you've decided to stay in your relationship, you will need to court acceptance every minute of the day until you are able to accept your relationship and your spouse just as they are. This is especially true if you've tried everything you know how, been to counseling more times than you can count, and realize that this is as good as it gets. If you have decided to stay then your task is really learning to accept your relationship just as it is.

Try accepting your spouse for who he is today.

Who he was when you met him is a memory. That is a cold hard fact. You may not even like him right now, but if you have decided to stay, you'll want to get to the business of accepting him and finding a way to like him and eventually love him. This might sound a little depressing, and I am sorry for that, as I have been there and I know how it feels. Still, there is a beauty in deciding to stay in a marriage when you know that it is not all you'd like it to be. I was married for 15 years and I was unhappy for several years; but I stayed, mostly because I believe in keeping my commitments. I was also very comfortable with the lifestyle that I had for me and my children, and my husband was a good provider and wonderful father. When I did finally leave, I knew I had done my best, and felt proud of the number of years that I had devoted to the relationship with the father of my children.

So try to accept where you are in your relationship, right now today. Accepting does not mean loving or even liking it, but just accepting. One thing that really helped me is the following prayer:

God, grant me the serenity to accept the things I cannot change, the courage to change the things I can, and the wisdom to know the difference.

-ANONYMOUS

Try saying this prayer every morning silently before you get up.

You might also try giving gratitude for the areas of your life that are working. Making a gratitude list every night before you go to bed can help as well. The important thing is that you have decided to stay, and you'll need to find peace and acceptance no matter what is going on in your relationship. Your acceptance and gratitude will give you a sense of serenity that can carry you through even the most difficult times in your marriage. There is power in making a decision and deciding to stay is an honorable decision. There is also, always, the hope that things will improve, but even if they don't you will be in a place of peace and acceptance knowing that you made a conscious decision to stay.

In *The Power of Now,* Eckhart Tolle advocates learning to accept a situation, as though you chose the situation. This is empowering, because it helps eliminate that feeling of hopelessness. It also frees you up to find some happiness in your relationship as it exists today, rather than on focusing on what you'd like to change about your mate in some imagined perfect future. All we have is now, so if you can learn to embrace the now, you'd be surprised at how your view of your relationship will change.

Another important part of acceptance is to stop comparing your relationship to that of others. Sure, your best friend Heather's husband may take her to dinner every Tuesday and shower her with gifts, but remember you only know what Heather shares with you. You really don't know what someone's relationship is like—so please don't compare. It's also important to ignore the picture-perfect relationships you see on television or in the movies. There are no perfect relationships and what works for one couple may be a disaster for another couple. Don't let anyone set the benchmark for you—not society, not your mama, your sister, or Hollywood. Your relationship is your relationship. So please just accept and appreciate your man for who and whatever he is, because with all his quirks and imperfections he's yours, and that is something to be thankful for.

19

LEARN TO LOVE YOUR MAN AGAIN

To love is a verb. Love can be a feeling as well, but we are talking about the verb in this section; the act of love. If you are going to stay you will want to learn actively to love your man on a consistent basis.

Every man is different, so you will need to get back to the business of getting to know your man again. You will want to specially tailor your love style to your partner's particular needs and tastes, at least sometime. Once you know who he is, then you will be able to love him in a way that he feels loved. It's easy to love people the way that we want to be loved ourselves. After all, that's what we are comfortable with. But, there is something special about loving someone in a way that they feel loved; it sends a message that you really care, and you took the time to find out what is important to your man. That's what a lover does.

Because you have decided to stay, you'll need to learn about him—even on the days when you can't stand him. The best way to learn about him, no matter how much you think you know him, is to really listen to him. Find ways to listen to him, and then respond with loving acts, consistently. You could always ask him what he wants, but there is something exceptional about a person who loves us so much that they take the time to know who we are and what makes us happy and then responds accordingly. For example, if you know he's interested in cars then get him a ticket to NASCAR, a car show, or buy a subscription to a car magazine for him. It does not cost money to love. Another idea is to fix his favorite food, and have the house stocked with his favorite wine or beer. I remember some years ago asking a male cousin what I could get my husband for Christmas. I will never forget his response, because he said, simply—A blow job! It was clear what he wanted from his wife.

There is beauty in the act of loving because you are showing that it is okay to be vulnerable. This will eventually cause your man to warm up to you in ways you hadn't thought possible. You will also get a tremendous sense of calm and control knowing that you took the initiative to please him.

List some activities you can do this week to love your man in a manner that he will understand and appreciate:

1.

2.

3.

Once you know what you need to do, go forward and take the steps to love him. You might even start by recommitting to him. One idea is to take some time at night, right before you go to bed when the lights are off and the room is quiet, tell him that you love him, always have, and always will. Look deep into his eyes, and then give him the best sex he's ever had.

TURN YOUR BEDROOM INTO A LOVE NEST

If you are going to stay, you will need to bring out the big guns. Start by making sure he understands you mean business, in a good way. You really want to have a place where the two of you can reconnect and de-stress. Your bedroom should feel like a vacation for the two of you, a place where you are kind to one another and can talk about anything.

Here are some tips for turning your bedroom into a love nest

1. Paint the room a calm color, one that soothes the two of you. One idea is to use spa-like colors to help set a relaxing mood.
2. Remove all electronics, except for the radio. I know this is hard, but the bedroom should be

for sleeping or making love. Make sure that it is conducive to that.

3. Buy a CD player and have CDs filled with music that mean something to the two of you. Don't hesitate to add a little Francis Cabrel's "Je t'aimais, je t'aime, je t'aimerai." This is the most romantic song on earth. Its title means, "I have loved you. I love you. I will love you."
4. Make sure your mattress is very comfortable and of a quality that suits both of you well. If it is not, then please—please—get a new one.
5. Re-do your bed and make it like the hotel beds by layering quality neutral colored bed linens. You might even try a heated mattress pad if you live in a cold climate. Layer the linens by placing the cotton blanket over the flat sheet, then the comforter, then another flat sheet, all topped with a cotton blanket. I'm telling you, it will feel like you are in a hotel room every night. You'll need a down alternative comforter, spa pillows, 400 count sheets, high-quality cotton blankets and a 400-count mattress pad.
6. Get rid of any bright lights. Add low lights to set a calm mood.
7. Get the children into their own beds. Believe me, kids in the marital bedroom is a recipe for disaster. Learn and practice every trick in the book to get your children sleeping in their own beds. Aside from the obvious, you need to get your sleep. There's no way

you can have a happy relationship if you are sleep deprived, let alone sex deprived.
8. Never, never argue in the bedroom. If you need to argue, do it elsewhere. This one is pretty self-explanatory.
9. Clean, dust, and organize the room. Make sure there is no visible clutter, even if it means putting a cloth over all that stuff on your husband's dresser. Nothing causes stress like visible clutter. Do what you can to organize. Get a chest for all those blankets, get a basket for magazines and bins for miscellaneous items. Put as many things in your closet or in other areas of the house as you can. The idea is to create a calming environment.
10. Get a tray for drinks and light snacks. Imagine just the two of you in your cozy room sharing a glass of wine and nibbling on some cheese together. What a way to end a day!
11. Get room-darkening shades or curtains. The room should be completely dark for sleeping. The dark can really relax the two of you and create more intimacy. You will also wake up better rested.

Put these tips into practice and honor your bedroom. You will be glad you did.

GET CLOSER

Even if you are distant from your spouse and you are not talking, take the initiative to get closer to one another. You've got to start somewhere, so here are some ideas:

1. Dance to your wedding song right there in your living room—just grab him and dance. It's free and its fun.
2. Laugh together. If it's been awhile since you two laughed, then rent a funny movie, or get to a comedy club, but please laugh. Laughter can heal just about anything and will bring you closer.
3. Reinvent date night. You don't have to spend $50 for a sitter and $100 on dinner, just get the kids to bed and head to your bedroom with a bottle of wine, and some real good take out.
4. Get a hotel. Every few months or so, go to a hotel together on a weekday.

There is just something so sexy about this. Check in early and stay until it's time to pick up the kids.

5. Cook together. There is something sensual about creating a meal together. If your guy is a horrible cook, let him read you a recipe, or stir the risotto, or pour the wine. Just get him involved in the kitchen.
6. Feed him. If it's beer and buffalo wings he loves, stock up your fridge with these items every once in a while. Having his favorite foods on hand will remind him of how much he means to you and that you desire to please him.
7. Go to a spa for the day. You can get a

wonderful couple's package for about $300 if you shop around. You might even be able to get a massage therapist to come to your home.
8. Give each other a hot stone massage. A hot stone massage is relaxing, calming, and healing.
9. Take a hike on a rocky trail. Find a local trail, get a group of friends together and go hiking. This can really bring you together, especially if the trail is challenging, because you will need to rely on each other and take care of each other as you climb. This kind of activity can bring you closer.
10. Read to each other. Take some time to just sit and read to one another.
11. Compliment your mate, hug him and tell him you love him every single day. In time, you will feel the positive vibes come back to you, if not immediately.
12. Listen to your partner. Just listen with all your senses, even if he talks about work the whole time.
13. Make love every night for a week. That's right, give it up. You'll be glad you did.
14. Write him a love note and leave it on his dresser. This can be a real ice- breaker for you two.
15. Take the children to a friend's house, go back home, and play a game of butt-naked "tag."
16. The next time he gets ready to leave the house, take a look at him and imagine that there is a possibility that you may never see

him again. Then kiss him with that thought in mind. Try doing this every time he leaves the house. You will find that things get lighter between you.

MAKE YOUR MARRIAGE A PRIORITY

This is the time to pay attention to your relationship. You may have other things going on, but you really must carve out the time to get your relationship back to where you want it so that you are happy, or at least content with your decision to stay.

Here are some tips for taking your relationship from good to great!

1. When your husband is home, pay attention to him. This means listen to him if he's talking; don't paint your nails or watch television while he's talking, even if you are sick of hearing about his job, football, or cars.

2. Hire a sitter just because, whether you have plans or not. Sometimes couples just need to be together alone in order to reconnect.

3. Cut back on activities that take you away from home. This doesn't mean that you have to give up the things that bring you joy, but you really want to put your all into your relationship until it is sailing along as smooth as possible. If you talk

with your girlfriends or your mother every night, limit it to maybe a few times a week or to the times when your spouse is not at home.

4. Work from home a few days a week if you can. This will make a big difference because you will find that you are significantly less stressed and have more energy for your family. When you are relaxed, you can handle just about anything.

5. Spend 20 minutes each week writing about your deepest thoughts and feelings regarding your relationship. Ask your partner to participate as well.

6. Try a new activity with your partner. It could be something as simple as trying a new board game or learning a new skill together. Just about anything different will help you connect in a different way.

Don't File For Divorce Just Yet

20

COMMUNICATION

You've heard it a thousand times, but communication really is the key to a healthy relationship. I know it gets tough sometimes to listen to your spouse, especially after you have had a hard day, but it's critical to listen often and attentively if you want to stay together. If he's venting about work, traffic, or his car, just lend an ear. Be sure to listen enough to ask questions. By asking questions, you really let him know that you have heard him and what he has said is important. Be patient and don't interrupt, no matter how tempted you may be. If you're busy, stop what you are doing if you can—if not, carve out time for him later in the evening. Good communication starts with listening.

Another way to keep the lines of communication open is by being honest. This is the man you married. Don't be afraid to open up to him. It can only create more intimacy between the two of you. Be vulnerable and bare your soul to him. Don't be embarrassed or ashamed at losing face. Let him know that you trust him enough to tell him your deepest truths. If you are lucky, he too will open up and you will share an intimacy you only dreamed about.

In addition to listening and being honest, you'll want to set a tone of respect when you communicate. Even if you are used to saying "fuck you" to each other, stop the pattern. Whatever the issue is, whether someone walks away, hangs up, or just tunes out, stop the pattern. You can't control what your spouse does, but you can be respectful.

If things are really heated, text or send emails when you calm down. This works wonders for a friend of mine. Whenever she and her husband have a spat, and they aren't speaking, he will send a text to break the ice. Once he sent her the most beautiful love song and nothing more. The song was his effort to apologize and save face. The love song made her all mushy and she had no problem calling him.

Eventually, your partner will follow your lead and your conversations will regain their civility.

PART IV

UNCOUPLING

I remember being curled up in a ball holding my young son as he sobbed uncontrollably on the bathroom floor. My heart still breaks. There are no words for this type of pain.

Do not take separating lightly.

Don't File For Divorce Just Yet

UNCOUPLING

I can honestly say that deciding to leave my marriage was the most difficult part of the divorce process. I often likened it to how the space shuttle must feel when it comes through the fiery atmosphere after spending all that time in the comfort and solitude of space. Like the shuttle, it seemed like forever before my feet would touch the ground and I was safely back to earth.

I am a very sensitive person and had felt unloved in my relationship for a number of years. I now know that the lack of love I felt was not all due to my first husband's personality, but due in part to me not knowing how to love myself and not expressing my love for God. No one can do without love—love of God, love of self, and love of others. My lack of self-love did me in.

I wondered how I would find the strength to leave my marriage? How could I go one day without seeing my babies, who were nine and ten at the time? I was scared beyond belief, but I knew that I would surely wind up in a mental institution or an alcoholic if I didn't take steps to change my life. I'm not exaggerating. Really, I had seen too many women in my hometown end up alcoholics because they stayed in unhappy marriages. My saving grace was my children. I knew I had to get myself together for them.

This section is for any woman who has decided to take the path of divorce. It contains what I learned and what I know now. God bless you, and I pray you find my words to be of use.

21

EMOTIONS

No one can possibly tell you how you will feel as you take this journey to uncouple. I can only share with you what I felt, and what I learned.

Denial—it was the first emotion I felt when I decided to separate from my first husband. Just eight months prior to separating from my husband, I was in big-time denial that there were any problems in my relationship. I walked around telling myself that everything was perfect in my marriage. Much of the time I even convinced myself that the relationship was perfect, because if I believed there were problems I would be forced to take some kind of action. A close friend later told me she knew things weren't perfect between us simply because I insisted things were "perfect." My friend had been married long enough to know there are hiccups in even the best long-term relationships.

Fear caused most of my denial. I was afraid of how I felt about my marriage, so I was scared out of my wits to examine my feelings. My emotions were my boogey monster. As a girl, I never really learned how to access, identify, or process my emotions. So my level of denial actually served to protect me from emotions that were foreign to me.

During my marriage, few things frightened me more than my own emotions. I'd given them some kind of power over me, which made denial necessary for me to function. I came out of my state of denial when I went into a deep depression, which I now know was brought on, partially, by low estrogen levels caused by peri- menopause. The rest of the depression was due to burnout—just being worn down.

The depression, unlike any I had ever experienced before or since, led me to a psychologist. It was in the process of therapy when I discovered that I was in denial about my relationship. I can still see the therapist's face when she asked me about my ex. "So, how are things between you and your husband?" she asked. I responded, "Great."

"How is your husband?" she probed further. "Great," I said again. After months of therapy I was ready to address marital issues and ready to make a decision whether I was going to try to fix the issues between my then-husband and myself.

As for the depression, thank God it lifted after a couple of months. It would be several more months before I discovered the low estrogen levels, but that's another story. I guess they call it the change of life for a reason.

Once I was out of denial, boy did the emotions come flowing out. I cried tears, tears, and more tears. I read ferociously during this time, trying desperately to access and identify the emotions

I was feeling. Learning to identify and feel my emotions was like learning a foreign language. Two books were of great help to me during this time: Judith Orloff's Emotional Freedom, and Raphael Cushnir's The One Thing Holding You Back. These books were invaluable because they helped me identify my emotions and really got at the underlying issues in my marriage and within myself. The books were life changers for me.

I also prayed for clarity at the local Catholic church several times a week. Clarity eventually came in the form of a low-dose birth control pill which helped my hormone levels so that I really could think clearly. Thank God for my doctor at Johns Hopkins, and the kindness of nurse Paula who has seen me through two miscarriages, two beautiful sons, a stuck IUD (and I mean STUCK), and peri-menopause.

Relief was the first emotion I felt after I decided to leave. I felt free and I knew, instinctively, for me, I was making the right decision. I felt like I was waking up and it was spring. I felt so alive again, as though I had been sleeping and now I was alive. I think I felt that way because, on a number of different levels, I was previously stuffing my feelings down instead of dealing with them.

After I accepted the fact that I wanted a divorce, and we were going to get divorced, I began to feel a load off my shoulders. I suddenly felt freer and lighter. I felt great. I began looking forward to my new life, although I still had a lot of fear about how the children would fare and how I would survive on my own.

It didn't help that my ex-husband decided to get the courts involved. He was bullying me and I knew it. It was an awful, awful time. He got a lawyer and immediately filed a nonsense motion in court. It was a scare tactic designed to punish me for wanting out of our marriage. We eventually decided on joint physical and legal custody of our boys, but believe me he made it extremely difficult for me.

EMOTIONS

It was during this time that I knew I'd made the right decision to leave. By getting the lawyers involved, he woke me up; after all I am a lawyer. It hit home that I had to protect myself and my children at all costs. I had to get tough, but at the same time I needed this to be a civil divorce. I would have it no other way. My kids deserved that, and it was in their best interests. Despite how angry I was, and I was angry, I had to find a way to get past my anger, deal with my first husband's anger, and find a way to come together for the sake of the children.

No it wasn't all peaches and cream after that. Guilt soon crept in, little by little. I felt guilty because I wondered whether I had done all I could do to save my marriage. I felt guilty over a failed relationship. I felt guilty over fracturing my family. This felt terribly, terribly selfish. These emotions were a surprise to me. I felt like I had failed terribly.

This wasn't true either, quite the contrary.

Many acquaintances asked how I could leave my marriage. As a result of their questions, I felt even guiltier. My friends, on the other hand, were very supportive of my decision, whether they understood it or not. Still I felt the grief and the tremendous sadness of something ending. It was a loss, a big one. It was also a beginning though. This was something I would realize after that long winter I described at the beginning of this book.

Was there more that I could have done? Looking back, I did my best and it was time to move on. In time I came to accept that. Believe me, I hoped during this period that all our problems would go away and that things would be right between us again, but the reality is that we'd given it our best shot. We were married for over a decade and had been to counseling several times. We'd tried, we just were not compatible and had grown too far apart.

We parted ways in the fall. I was running on sheer adrenaline during this time, never knowing what was going to happen next, and not really sure of what steps to take. The only thing that kept me going was my children. I knew I owed it to them to work with their dad. After all, no matter how I felt about him, the children love their dad, and I had to accept that. I was determined not to make them suffer for how I felt about him. We had an arrangement that worked for both of us and the children. I felt a tremendous sense of accomplishment and freedom. I felt so free.

My sense of freedom soon turned to loneliness. I was not used to being alone. I didn't even know what it was like to be lonely, but fortunately I learned that alone did not mean lonely. After all, I was truly blessed with several friends who were there for me. Friends who listened to me for months, who held me and told me it would be all right, and that I would be fine. I am eternally grateful for these friends and would never ever have been able to get through that tough period without them.

There were also periods when I thought of going back, running like crazy to the safety of my marriage. These feelings were short lived, and came mostly during that big snow storm, on those cold lonely winter nights, or whenever I had a crisis. Whenever the crisis was gone, so was my desire to go back to my marriage. Looking back, I think I was just scared to go forward. I had no idea what was ahead of me. I was also grieving for our family unit. This was natural, I suppose; we'd been together for so long. Uncoupling was not easy, but I never went back because I would have been running from something, instead of to something. Nope, I had to find my courage, and in time, I did.

Eventually, I got to a point where I began to work on myself. I must have read every book I could find on self-discovery. I began to learn about me, what I liked, what I wanted, how I thought—all things me. It was this search for myself that led me to embrace where I was and learn that I was right where I was supposed to be.

Then there was the issue of facing life alone without a mate. I felt that I would become a spinster at 45 and be alone forever, never to date again. This was False Evidence that Appeared Real (FEAR) at its finest. I joined every Internet dating site I could find, only to find fault with every suitor that dared to step forward, and boy did they step forward.

I was not ready to date though. This should have been no surprise. What it did tell me was that men would be there when I was ready. I had always had relationships, and had no real reason to believe that this would not be the case once I had spent time healing from my marriage. For a while I wanted to get married right away, convinced I couldn't do this on my own, and wanting to run to the safe haven of another partner. This was just fear talking though.

What I know now is that it is wisest to wait a month for every year that you were married, before you begin dating. This is hard. You will be lonely, that is a fact. But if you can wait to date, you will attract a much more desirable and healthier partner because you will have allowed yourself to heal from the inside out.

These are all the emotions I felt, every one of them. You know the beauty of all this was that I finally learned to identify and express my emotions. It was a big leap for me to put my feelings in writing for the entire world, but it will be worth it if just one person learns from what I've been through.

Don't File For Divorce Just Yet

22

CHILDREN

Besides dealing with the emotional issues of divorce, the biggest challenge for me was making sure my children were healthy and that they got through this as whole and as intact as they were before. There is nothing more frightening than the thought of someone trying to get custody of your children, whether it is just a fear or a reality. Realistically, custody is an issue that you will likely face if you have children.

I can't say what is best for your family, only that children benefit from a mother and a father. If you keep this on your mind as you move forward, you will make the right decisions for you and your children. That was my premise in deciding how to parent my children through this divorce. I wanted my children to have the benefit of two parents who loved them very much, even if we didn't all live in the same home any longer. They deserved that much. Even though I wanted to move as far away from their dad as possible, I knew that in the end the children would suffer. They were used to seeing him and they loved him. Their relationship with him had not changed, mine had, and I wasn't going to make them suffer for our decisions.

As I mentioned earlier, we decided on joint legal and physical custody which we reached through an agreement with our lawyers. We are lucky in that we can work together. We talk frequently and are both involved in the children's lives. When we are too angry to talk, we send emails or letters in the mail—anything to avoid an argument. I am proud of where we ended up in terms of how we parented them through this process.

My advice as a mother and lawyer is that you get an attorney, and make your divorce as amicable as possible for the sake of your children. If you have children, you cannot afford to go through this process without a lawyer. Gone are the days that mothers are automatically given sole custody of the kids and the dads pay child support. You have to work with these men; after all they are the fathers. To our kids and the courts, their roles are just as important as that of the mothers.

Getting a solid custody arrangement for your child should be your first priority. You should have this in place before you move out. It will give you a sense of peace and provide continuity for your children. Then you can deal with all the other issues of divorce, which I will discuss later.

Aside from the custody issue, the other big issue with the children was telling them about the separation. This fear loomed heavy on us for months, but eventually their dad and I got together, agreed on what we'd say, and told the boys that we were separating. He did the talking. He said we had tried very hard, but that we just were not happy and could no longer make it work. The children cried, and my heart broke into a thousand tiny pieces. I had never felt so raw and helpless emotionally. I remember being curled up in a ball holding my young son as he sobbed uncontrollably on the bathroom floor. My heart still breaks. There are no words for this type of pain. Do not take separating lightly.

We made it through that night. I got the boys a counselor and alerted the school psychologist to enlist her help for when they returned to school. I also got them a dog, the same night we told them about the pending divorce. A little white Shitzhu named Jake. I took my oldest son with me along for the ride to pick up the dog from a breeder about an hour and half away from where we lived. It was a long dark ride through rural Maryland. I remember my son saying he was very upset about our pending separation but that he felt much better knowing that we had so many things organized, like their schedule, and the fact that he would not change schools. I sighed in relief because it was the first sign that we would make it through this process. Then he said, "But Mom, a part of me will always be eternally sad." That broke my heart. Still I was amazed at the depth of my 10-year-old's thinking and his ability to comprehend this very adult situation we had put upon him.

Try to keep as much familiarity and routine in the children's lives as you can. Divorce can feel like a death of sorts. I hate to say that because it's also a beginning, but there is a tremendous sense of loss, even under the best circumstances. Your children will inevitably feel this loss, but you can help them by keeping their surroundings and schedule as familiar as possible. I recall being so desperate to change, to get out of my marriage, that I wanted everything to be new. This was just what I wanted.

CHILDREN

Fortunately, I loved my sons enough to put them first, and as a result I stayed in our town, kept them in the same school, and they had the same friends.

After you have developed a parenting plan, retained an attorney, and reached a custody arrangement with your spouse, you are ready to tell your children, to prepare to move out, and implement your custody agreement.

23

MOVING OUT

The most important point here is not to move out of that house without a separation agreement/child custody arrangement in place. You do not want your spouse going to court and saying that you abandoned the family. This may not go well for you. So meet with a lawyer to develop the separation/child custody agreement, get your spouse to sign it, and then get it entered into the court record. Don't be surprised if you can't get a custody order or separation agreement entered into the court record until you actually move out. The key here is to have it in place before you move out. Your lawyer can help you with this. If your spouse gives you a hard time, which he may, then have your lawyer and his remind him that if he goes before a judge he could end up with slim visitation rights and paying a lot of money in child support. Then make sure that what you are offering him is better.

Be fair, and make the offered agreement something that is best for everyone. No matter how mad your spouse is, he will likely come around if you are continuously fair throughout this process.

The important thing is that you do not leave your family home without having a signed document about who will take care of your children and how. That is your goal; keep it in the forefront of your mind and you will succeed.

In the state that we lived in, we had to be separated for a year before we could divorce. We decided to both move out of the home we were living in at the time and get new places. The weekend we moved, my mother came to help out. The weekend was extremely amicable and I was proud of that. It was conflict-free because we had a custody agreement in place, which was our biggest issue through the process. My mother kept the children while my ex-husband and I separated things and moved out.

It is unrealistic to think that everyone can uncouple this conflict free. So, I will tell you that it is very important that you do not tell a man you are leaving him and then stay in the house for months on end, like I did. My girlfriend's mother gave this advice to her, and she passed it along to me. I was lucky, but the advice is true. You never know how someone will behave when you tell them you are leaving them. People change when they are about to lose something as sacred as a wife. Another friend called religiously to ensure that I was not buried in the backyard. Fear would get the best of her when she did not hear from me after a few days.

Anyway, please have a plan in place, and hopefully even a place to live that is suitable for you and your children when you tell your spouse that you are leaving. If this is not possible, then at least move out of the bedroom into an area where you can have your privacy. I probably don't need to say this, but don't date during this time. If you are seeing someone cut if off until you get out of the house. Now is not the time to date; you'll want to focus on your children. Plus you probably won't be in the best shape to make relationship decisions. Besides, if the person you are seeing is worth keeping, he will wait until you get through this process.

MOVING OUT TIPS

1. Do a budget of how much money you need to live on—www.kiplinger.com has an excellent budget form that you can use. The site is also good for keeping abreast of money issues.
2. Determine how much money you need and set aside enough money for your move. You'll also want to have a small emergency fund before you leave. Emergencies will come up. Especially now because you won't be able to calculate exactly what your expenses are. This is a time to live frugally, at least for a short while anyway.
3. Begin planning your move at least three months in advance.
4. Move within your children's school district, so as not to disrupt their schedule and social life.
5. Take a second job if you need to make money before you move.

6. Do not publicize your move to anyone except your closest friends or family members.
7. Gather, buy, or borrow household items that you will need and store them away.
8. Buy at least one new item for your new house and keep it with you. I remember buying a kitchen rug and keeping it in the back of my trunk. This rug reminded me of the new life that I was about to embark on.
9. Set up child care for your children during the move and a few days afterwards. As I mentioned, my mother came and stayed with us during the move. I would not have been able to get through any of it without her. She was a Godsend.
10. Go easy on yourself. It will all come together in time.

None of this is easy. I remember the last day of our move, when I looked back at the house and there were empty rooms where my family had been. I could almost touch the loss, sadness, and sense of failure. Still, as I left the house that November night, I somehow felt I was walking into a new beginning and the slightest hint of wonderment came over me.

24

FINANCES

Hopefully, you've got the money thing down and can skip this section. But, just in case you haven't, please read on.

The lessons I learned about money during my separation period were invaluable. It was important that I learned those lessons because money represents security. When you are out there on your own, you need security and the knowledge that you can manage your money and handle what life throws at you. Having this feeling of security can give you a sense of peace and make you more able to handle the issues that will crop up with your children and their dad during this period.

You don't have to be a millionaire to have financial security. You just have to practice sound financial management every day. So, here's some advice to get you there.

DEVELOP A SPENDING PLAN

A spending plan is just a plan for how you will spend your money. Learning about and developing a spending plan was the first step toward financial security for me. The spending plan I used was developed by MP Dunleavey in her book, Money Can Buy You Happiness.

The plan basically ensures that you are spending your money in a way that makes you happy. So, yes, how you spend your money can make you happy. For example, I noticed that I was spending a lot of money on eating out and processed food at lunch. We have the best Asian gourmet food bars in the country.

The problem was that I didn't have enough money to do what I loved—travel. So, once I was aware of my pattern, I cut back on the convenience food and started putting the money away towards a vacation. I also cut back in other ways and redirected my money to make sure that I was getting what I wanted from my hard-earned money.

Before developing your spending plan, you will want to take a few weeks and examine where your money is going. The easiest way I found to do this is with PNC's Virtual Wallet Account. You can visit www.pnc.com to find out more about this type of account. A Virtual Wallet account will show you:

1. How much money you have on hand to spend every day.
2. How much money you have spent on any given day.

A bird's-eye view of your money and spending habits are crucial when trying to get a handle on spending. Besides PNC, there is also Quicken.com and Mint.com. Quicken costs money and was a bit complicated for me, but it's been around for years and many people swear by it. You can also link your Quicken account to several banks to get the same effect that you would get with a PNC Virtual Wallet account. Mint.com is also an excellent tool, and it's free. The only warning about Mint.com is that my experience has been that the information is not always up to date in terms of how much money you have and how much money you are spending. Perhaps this feature will improve in the future, so I'd recommend at least giving it a try, since it's free.

Now that you know how you are spending your money, you are ready to develop your spending plan. The plan is simple—you make sure that sixty percent of your bi-weekly net income goes to your primary bills such as rent, insurance, food, utilities and debt repayment. Then spend 10 percent on entertainment, 10 percent on long-term savings like retirement, 10 percent on short-term savings and 10 percent on long-term savings.

Use the spending plan as a guide. You may not be able to fund it all at once, but at least you have something to work towards. You will feel more in control just knowing that.

It is also very important that you follow some basic financial rules during this process. Always, always pay your basic bills first. That means your rent, lights, gas, car insurance, and telephone. You do not want to come home one day and find that you forgot to pay the light bill. This is not a good story for your children to tell their dad, or teachers for that matter.

After setting up your basic bills, you will want to set aside some money in an emergency fund. This is critical because you will have emergencies and you will not have a second income to help you. I did this by setting up a savings account online at www.smartypig.com. Smarty Pig is a great tool because you can use it to set up multiple savings goals and have the money taken directly from your savings or checking account. For example, I set up the following goals:

1. Emergency Fund—   goal = $2,000

2. Vacation Fund   —   goal = $750

3. School Clothes   —   goal = $300

4. Christmas Fund   —   goal = $500

Once my goals were set up, I determined when I'd like to accomplish them. I also factored the date into determining how much money I would have deducted each pay check. For example, I'd have $75 deducted bi-weekly until I reached my Emergency Fund goal. You can guess why I funded my Emergency Fund prior to funding any other goals. Ideally, you'd have at least three to six months of income set aside in an emergency fund, but that is not always possible. So, at a minimum strive to have one month of living expenses in there.

Additionally, you're going to want to make sure you have a repair warranty for your car, rental insurance, home appliance insurance, short term disability (or sick leave), gap insurance for your vehicle and umbrella insurance, and obviously medical insurance for you and your children. These types of insurance protections are really important, in addition to your Emergency Fund.

Prior to reaching my Emergency Fund goal, there were also times when I needed the money quickly. The fastest way to get my money through Smarty Pig was to edit a goal, any goal, stop the contributions, and then request to have the funds sent back to my checking account. If I used this process, then I typically had my money in my bank account within two days of making the request. The key here though is to edit the goal or fully fund the goal. This is pretty easy because you can always transfer money between goals.

Using Smarty Pig was a great way for me to put money aside to have when I really needed it. There are many ways to set money aside. Here are a few ideas:

1. Put money on a gift card and then put the gift card in a safe deposit box at home or at the bank.

2. Put a limited amount of cash in a steel security box at home ($500 max.).

3. Put the money in a cashier's check in your name and then store it at the bank in a safe deposit box.

These are just a few ideas that can help you to set aside your money, because emergencies will always crop up. Knowing that I had some money, even if it wasn't a lot, gave me an invaluable sense of security. Having a sense of security gave me confidence and strength as I went about rebuilding my new life.

Another important issue for me as I went through this process was prioritizing the money. Fortunately, I had enough money to live on, but the issue was how to spend it wisely. Because I no longer had two incomes, I really had to prioritize my expenses and get smart about money. The most helpful way I've found is to categorize how I was going to spend my money.

CATEGORY 1 BILLS

Emergency Fund

CATEGORY 2 BILLS

School Loans

CATEGORY 3 BILLS

Medical Bills
Housing—Rent or Mortgage
Credit Card Payments
Legal Bills
Gas & Electricity
Other Bills
Water Bill
Car Payment
Car Insurance

Once I categorized the bills, I then put them into a three-part plastic container with three separate bins. As my bills came in, I'd open them and put the Category 1 Bills in the top bin, the Category 2 Bills in the second bin, and the Category 3 Bills in the third bin. Then every Saturday I'd spend about 30 minutes opening any bills I'd received that week and ensuring that they were scheduled for payment through my online bill payment system at my bank. I'd schedule the bills based on my paycheck, always making sure the Category 1 Bills were paid first. After that I'd disperse the money between my Category 2 and 3 bills. This is not the only way to manage money, but it is has worked wonders for me because it's not complicated and, except for checking my account daily and making sure my bills are paid, there really isn't much for me to do.

25

LEGAL-EAZE

The best piece of advice that I can give you is to GET A LAWYER! I'm a lawyer (if I haven't said that enough already throughout this book) and I did what? I got a lawyer! I was in no condition to represent myself. Fortunately, I recognized that early on. I knew I needed someone to help me through this process, and that for the sake of my children, failure was not an option. My kids were involved, and like most mothers, my kids are everything to me.

CONTAINING YOUR LEGAL COSTS

1. Shop around. Expect to pay about $100 to $200 per hour, and $1,000 for each court appearance. Obviously this fee will vary depending on the lawyer you select, whether your divorce is contested, and your geographical location.
2. Be civil to your partner. Not only is it the right thing to do, it will save you money and eliminate a lot of stress. If the two of you work together your court costs will be lower, as he will not be dragging you in to court every time

you sneeze. It doesn't matter if you fought every day while you were married. Forget it. At this moment, it's about your well-being, the kids, and your money.

3. Ask your lawyer to let you know every time he is about to incur a cost on your account. For example, I had no idea that my lawyer was calling my first husband's lawyer and running up the costs for both of us. At 30 minutes a phone call, that translated to $100 per phone call. This really jacked up my bill. Of course I knew lawyers can be expensive, but in the midst of everything this was not on my radar screen.
4. Try to get a set cost before hiring the lawyer, even if you pay an initial retainer.
5. Keep your initial retainer as small as possible, around $500.
6. Develop your own settlement agreement with your partner, then have your lawyer review it.
7. If you have trouble reaching an agreement, which you likely will, conduct mediation with your lawyer, your partner, and his lawyer. This will help flesh out the issues, and could avoid any need for a $1,000 court appearance. Keep this meeting to two or three hours. If one of you is being unreasonable, it will come out in this meeting. Nobody likes to be embarrassed so you'd be surprised how this one meeting can work wonders.
8. At all costs, avoid the court, if possible, except to file your settlement agreement and get the

final divorce. The courts should be a last resort, because you do not want a third party deciding how you and your children are going to live.

PREPARE A DRAFT SEPARATION AGREEMENT

The first step to getting what you want is knowing what you want.

Drafting your own agreement is critical because it will guide you when working with your partner and with your lawyer. It does not have to be perfect, that's what lawyers are for. Right now all you need is a pen, a couple of sheets of paper, and some ideas about what you want. This exercise is solely to get you focused on areas that you will need to consider.

A draft separation agreement can also serve as a compass, but ultimately you will need to have your lawyer review the document and make sure that it fully represents your interests within the confines of the law of your particular state.

Here is a list of areas you'll want to include in your separation agreement:

1. Child Custody
   Most mothers instinctively want sole custody. However, judges aren't as apt today to award mothers sole custody. Know this going in and be willing to work with your spouse on this issue.

In my case we have joint custody. I can say it is difficult because there are days when my children are not with me. This is hard, but fortunately they have a father who loves them as much as I do. So in that sense, I recognize that I am blessed. In our case, joint custody works well because we have, for the most part, always acted civilly towards each other for the sake of our children. Joint custody requires a lot of communication between the parents. You are both equally involved in making decisions for the children. If you keep the children at the forefront of your decisions, you will ultimately make the right call. If there is no abuse, children benefit from having the love of both parents. It can be hard at times, but I recognize that my sons need their dad as much as they need me.

2. Parenting Plan
The parenting plan is a plan or schedule that defines which parent will keep the children when. Start by making a schedule that involves as little shuffling of the children between parents as possible. Every situation is different and what you agree to early on may not be what you end up with. The physical and mental health of your children should be the guide in terms of whether your parenting plan is successful. Here are some examples:

a. Weekday/Weekends
   This plan involves the children staying with one parent during the week and the other parent for three weekends out of the month.
b. School Year/Summer Break
   With this plan the children will stay with one parent during the school year and the other over summer break. This works well if you and the children's father are in different states.
c. Weekday Split
   This is the plan that my children's father and I have. They are with each of us for about half the week. This is not what we started out with. We didn't want the children shifting back and forth so frequently, but ultimately, our children guided us and led us to an arrangement that works for all of us.

The key with any plan is flexibility and putting the interests of the children first. The plan you select will depend on the age and needs of your child. Please ensure that your parenting plan is consistent with the level of custody that you have been awarded by the court. For example, don't allow your spouse to see the kids 70 percent of the time when you have been awarded joint custody, unless it is in the best interests of your children, or you are 100 percent sure he will not drag you into court and request sole custody of your children.

3. Retirement
   Be sure that you get some of your spouse's future and current retirement payments, if in fact you are entitled to it. Your lawyer can advise you on this, but stay vigilant on the issue throughout the process.

4. Health Insurance
   You'll want to be clear on who will pay for health insurance for the children. In our case, my children's father covers the insurance premiums, while I am responsible for co-pays.

5. Beneficiary Information
   Remember to change your beneficiary information as soon as you can. You'll want to check with your employer. It's worth mentioning in the agreement so there are no misunderstandings.

6. Personal and Real Property
   Your lawyer should help you with this, but you can and should at least be clear about how you'd like to divide assets, keeping in mind the necessity to compromise.

7. Taxes
   You'll want to address how you will file your taxes. For example, will you begin to file as married filing separately prior to receiving the divorce decree?

This list is not meant to be exhaustive. At a minimum you'll want to address these areas, as well as any other issues that pertain to your particular situation. This is why it's so important to have a lawyer review the document, even before discussing it with your partner.

Once you know what you want, then you can decide whether to discuss the agreement with your spouse alone, or in the presence of your attorney. Please make this decision carefully as you are the only one who knows your particular situation and the temperament of the parties involved. In my case, I think we were both ready to get out of the marriage, so working together was a little easier than what might be usual for other couples. Really, we'd given it our best shot. This was not a Hollywood marriage. It lasted 15 years. It was my longest relationship. And, though it did not last a lifetime in the eyes of the law, he is the father of my children and will always be in my life.

So, yes, I accepted that I love him, still respect him, and am grateful to him for the role he plays as their dad. It took a long time to come to that realization because I think I believed I was not supposed to love and respect him still. That's just not in me. How do you "unlove" someone? Your relationship may change, but the love does not have to. Sure, relatives and friends may have decided to dislike your "ex" because of things you may have said in the past, but is it really in your best interest to carry around anger and pain for someone that you once loved and who may be the father of your children? I don't think so. Also, be very careful, because children pick up on conscious emotions and "unconscious" ones. So if you are carrying around unaddressed anger or resentment, your children are bound to act out these emotions in one way or another.

Besides, trying to unlove someone causes a lot of unnecessary pain. Coming to that realization has made working with my ex-husband substantially easier.

26

LEARNING TO LIVE AGAIN

After 14 years of being married, being single felt like I'd woken up in a new country where everyone spoke a different language. I felt so alienated at first, mostly because I was used to being part of a couple. It was a long six months before I felt totally comfortable on my own again. There was definitely some co-dependency going on for me, but I think that is the case in any long-term relationship to a certain extent.

I remember the first time I went out by myself to an event. The event was given by the International Club of D.C. The club was made up of professionals from around the globe who happened to be working in Washington, D.C. A friend from college told me about the group; she said she had met some wonderful people through the club. My first event was a Cherry Blossom Dance Festival at a hotel on Embassy Row. I was so excited to go, even though I had no idea what to expect. I went by myself. This didn't bother me, as I'd gone to school in Washington and worked there much of my adult life. So I felt somewhat comfortable. I had no idea what to wear, so I went with comfortable—a pair of jeans and a black shirt. Most women were in dresses and heels, but that was okay as it was a big deal for me just to be there on my own. Shortly after I arrived, another single woman, Kate, introduced herself. She was from Albania and was in Washington working for a national medical association. We made fast friends, and before you know it, we had several people asking us to dance. I turned them down for some reason. Had I forgotten how to dance? Who knows? I just wasn't comfortable cutting the rug with any of the potential suitors. I should have danced the night away because my only goal that night was to have fun.

I left the party early, even though I did not have to because my sons were with their father. As I drove home from the city to the suburbs, a sudden wave of loneliness hit me right there in my car. I started to cry. Looking back, I think I was just overwhelmed at having just gone out on the town on my own. The next day I was quite proud of myself. I recognized how brave I'd been by going to the party in the first place.

Despite my fears, that night was like a gateway—a huge door opener that created a chain of events. Here's how it went. Kate met a guy named Harry that night. Harry took Kate out to a Hookah club, just days before she caught him with another girl. Then Kate told me about the Hookah club in Arlington, VA. Next thing I knew, two Saturdays after the Cherry Blossom party, I was dancing it up at a Hookah club. If you don't know what a Hookah is, don't worry because neither did I until then. It's really just a fancy bong used mostly overseas. No, we were not smoking any illegal substances. In fact, I didn't even smoke the Hookah at all because I don't smoke and I have terrible allergies. In any case, the patrons at the club smoked flavored tobacco through the Hookah, or so I was told. Never mind the Hookah. That night at the club was magical. I danced the entire night away with a Greek guy who worked for a shipping company. At the end of the night he kissed my hand and that was it. That was perfect. God knows I was not ready for anything else. I came back to life that night right there in the Hookah club. After the club closed, Kate and I were invited to an after-party where we sang karaoke and ate pasta until 6 a.m. What a night, and all because I'd ventured out to that Cherry Blossom Festival party weeks before.

I'm still making my way, stumbling as I go. Since that time I have found a host of other things to do during the time that my sons are with their father. One night I sang karaoke in front of a hundred strangers at a local lounge. My singing voice was horrific. I'm still shocked that I pulled that one off. The hilarious thing is that the microphone wasn't on. So no one heard me squeak through one of Beyoncé's tunes. All that fear, for naught!

Then there was the night I wandered into a bridal shop and tried on wedding gowns. I got married on an island and had never tried on a white wedding gown. This was a hilarious evening. Then there was the time I signed up for Match.com only to find out that my ex was also on there. I am still in shock to this day about that one. Talk about strange. Then there was the time my mother set me up with her mail man. A very nice man, but I wasn't quite ready for a relationship. Yes, my antics are crazy. My co-workers say I should be writing a blog. I'm writing a book instead.

LEARNING TO LIVE AGAIN

One last word—whatever you do, do not jump right into another serious relationship. It is very tempting because you are used to being in a relationship, and relationships, good or bad, can provide some comfort. If you jump into another relationship right away without dating, you will miss a valuable opportunity for self-growth and exploration. I really don't want to get into the topic of dating, but I will say that God has not stopped making men and the next one you will meet is already here on earth. So there is no need to think for a minute that you will not have another husband or boyfriend if you choose. If you don't believe me, just post your picture on an Internet dating site. I was shocked at the number of available men. But, a word to the wise—some of these men, on the Internet, in your office, or at your gym, are predators just looking for women in a vulnerable emotional state. Please keep that in mind for your sake. It is tempting to date some of the handsome and available men that will come your way, but if you do, just make sure you have sharpened your people picking skills—otherwise you are likely to end up with someone who has the exact same qualities you may have disliked in your spouse. Believe me, these guys will come at you like they were chasing after Pac-Man. If you have been married for a long time, you are in no position to jump in the dating pool without having done your "self " work and your homework on these fellas. I also strongly advise not allowing any man to meet your kids until you've dated him for six months, met his family and friends, and seen how he treats children. Even then, it's not a good idea to have a man stay over until you know he's committed and worth keeping.

As hard as being single can be at times, it is also a blessing. It can be a time to sharpen your people-picker and to create the life you've always dreamed about. It's like starting with a blank slate on which you can write whatever you want. I can honestly say that I have learned more about myself in the last three years than at any other point in my life. I have finally gotten to know and love myself in ways I never even imagined.

The time in between relationships can be the best time of your life if you get out there and make the most of it. So use this time to do what you like and what you've never done before!

Don't File For Divorce Just Yet

What You Must Know First

www.ingramcontent.com/pod-product-compliance
Lightning Source LLC
Chambersburg PA
CBHW031352040426
42444CB00005B/255